Make Presentations with Confidence

Second Edition ◆ Vivian Buchan

Vivian Buchan is a writer and former faculty member at the University of Illinois and the University of Iowa. She has written extensively on many subjects and is the recipient of several honors and awards recognizing her work.

All inquiries should be addressed to:
Barron's Educational Series, Inc.
250 Wireless Boulevard
Hauppauge, New York 11788

Library of Congress Catalog Card No. 97-10352

International Standard Book No. 0-8120-9892-7

Library of Congress Cataloging-in-Publication Data
Buchan, Vivian.
   Make presentations with confidence / by Vivian Buchan. — 2nd ed.
    p. cm. — (Barron's business success series)
   ISBN 0-8120-9892-7
   1. Business presentations. I. Title. II. Series.
  HF5718.22.B83   1997
  658.4'52—dc21   97-10352
                                    CIP

PRINTED IN HONG KONG
98765432

Contents

◆

Part I

Getting Prepared
and Organized

Chapter 1

Foreword—
The Broad Picture:

What Communication Is All About

"The most immutable barrier in nature is between one man's thoughts and another's."

—William James

There's nothing mysterious about public speaking. Every time you open your mouth and someone listens, you are speaking in public. Presto! You are a public speaker. Although stage fright is the number one fear that keeps most people from speaking, it doesn't have to keep you sitting in an audience when you should be standing in front of one.

Every semester at the University of Iowa, a class of timid and reluctant students waited for me to wave a magic wand and turn them into competent speakers. They knew they had to pass a final exam by speaking in front of strange judges in an auditorium full of unfamiliar students before they could pass the course—required before they were allowed to graduate.

The exam was tough. They were allowed about half an hour to prepare a speech on an assigned topic, and were required to do it without using magazines or reference works. They were permitted to use only three small notecards as they gave their four-minute extemporaneous speeches.

I am happy to say none of my students ever failed to pass that final exam. The students were required to give eight four-minute extemporaneous speeches during the semester, which, though it prepared them to speak, isn't the same as years of experience. If those immature and insecure young freshmen could do it, think how much experience, maturity, and enthusiasm you bring to the situation.

When you see how the basic nuts and bolts of putting a speech together underpin the structure, and understand how to build on that foundation, you can speak with style and elegance anytime, anywhere.

THE TIES THAT BIND

Because I believe a speech can be no better than the speaker, it is important to become as "full" a person as possible, which is why some chapters deal with self-development. One of the most important truths you will ever learn is how our humanness binds us together. All people want much the same things out of life: health, happiness, prosperity, success, status, friends, family, love, and appreciation. When you realize people are more interested in themselves than anything else, you will have the key to unlocking their innermost needs and desires.

For example: You are reading this book hoping to get information that will help you become a poised and confident speaker. If the ideas I submit are inspiring and motivating, then I have communicated with you. We will have enjoyed an encounter that rewards us both.

This is communication at its best. For this brief time, we have touched each other in ways we hope will benefit us both.

Communication is not some mysterious process. It takes place when ideas from your mind are transferred to another's and arrive intact, complete, and coherent. The exchange takes place on a two-way highway with messages flowing in both directions. Both the sender and the receiver share the responsibility of making this transfer of ideas effective and satisfying.

Oratory is not communication. Finley Peter Dunn, an early 20th century humorist, said, "A man never becomes an orator if he has anything to say."

Sir Winston Churchill expressed his opinion of orators: "They can best be described as [people] who, before they get up, do not know what they are going to say; when they are speaking, do not know what they are saying; and, when they have sat down, do not know what they have said."

You are charged with a serious responsibility as a speaker. The Reverend Jenkin Lloyd Jones, a Welsh author, said, "The man who makes a bad thirty-minute speech to two hundred people wastes only a half hour of his own time. But he wastes one hundred hours of the audience's time—more than four days—which should be a hanging offense."

So you'll never be guilty of such an offense, let's get started finding out how to make effective presentations and do it as a poised and confident presenter who knows exactly what you're doing—and why.

Chapter 2

Finding Your Purpose:

Answer, "Why?" with, "Because…"

"The first thing in life to do is to do with purpose what one proposes to do."

—Pablo Casals

Confident speakers who appear to be organized and in control of their material *are* organized and in control. You don't start out on a trip without knowing where you're going, how to get there, and what you'll do when you arrive. You need a map to get you started and see that you arrive without getting lost or delayed along the way.

To present a successful speech, you need a map to (1) introduce your subject, (2) develop your material, and (3) reach a conclusion.

I call this map the "Why-and-Because Guide" that gets you started, keeps you going, and successfully takes you to a destination. And lets you do it with poise and confidence.

If I were to ask, "Did you have a good time on your vacation in Maine?" and you answered, "No, it was a total disaster," you would be expressing an opinion.

Then I might ask "Why? What happened?" and you might reply "The cottage was a mess, the neighbors drove us crazy, and everything was so expensive we couldn't afford any entertainment."

This conversation could be the format for a five-minute extemporaneous speech or a thirty-minute presentation at a seminar.

A simple four-line outline would look like this:

> SUBJECT: *Our vacation in Maine was a disaster. (Why)*
>
> BODY: (Because) *1. The cottage was a mess.*
> *2. The neighbors drove us crazy.*
> *3. Everything was too expensive.*
>
> CONCLUSION: *For these reasons, our vacation was an experience I never want to repeat.*

Knowing firsthand so much about this vacation, you could give a speech without referring to notes. But let's suppose you're still terrified to face an audience and positive you won't remember anything. Let's take the skeleton outline and dress it up with examples:

> SUBJECT: *Our vacation in Maine was a disaster.*

BODY: (Because) 1. The cottage was a mess:
a. The screens were full of holes.
b. The "spacious fireplace" had a broken damper and wouldn't work, so we sat wrapped in blankets to eat our "romantic" meals.
c. The "panoramic view" opened on junk cars and the windows were so dirty we couldn't see out.
2. The neighbors drove us crazy:
a. They fought day and night and yelled at their kids and dogs, who yelled right back at them.
b. They ran in and out without knocking to borrow ice cubes and food they never returned.
c. They came in late at night, revving the engine of their beat-up car right outside our bedroom window.
3. Everything was so expensive we couldn't go anyplace:
a. The bars had exorbitant cover charges and poor entertainment.
b. The amusement park

> *rides were rickety as well*
> *as expensive.*
>   c. *A boat cost fifty dollars a*
>   *day, so we only took one*
>   *out one day.*
> CONCLUSION: *A simple repetition of the three*
>   *main ideas is enough to make a*
>   *satisfying conclusion.*

YOUR OUTLINE IS AN AUTOMATIC PILOT

A simple organization is enough to keep even the most inexperienced and timid speaker on course. It will act as a guidance system that will keep you on course and bring you in for a perfect landing. Too many speakers fail to make a satisfying conclusion. They move from one point to the next, and when they've explored them all, they just stop. They abandon their speeches instead of concluding them. The listeners wonder what the speaker did (or didn't) do that left them feeling bewildered and shortchanged.

A speech is like a baseball diamond. It has a home plate and three bases. When you hit a home run, you leave home plate, race around the bases, and come in for a score. You do the same thing with a speech: You start, move through your "becauses," and get back home with your conclusion.

GETTING FROM START TO FINISH

When driving, you use directional signals to alert other motorists as to what you intend to do. In a speech, you use transitions to keep your audience informed and with you. Transitions do five things in a speech:

1. *Change direction*

2. *Add something new*

3. *Elaborate on an idea*

4. *Digress from the main topic*

5. *Move into a new idea*

Moving from your introduction (discussed later) into your first "because," you can use these transitions: "In the first place..." "Most important..." "First let me explain..." or "My first point..."

Going on to the next "because," you can say "In the second place..." "Next..." "In addition..." or "Also..."

Moving into the third "because," you can say "Last but no less important..." "Finally..." or "My third reason..."

Transitional connectives have four major classifications: (1) to introduce, (2) to add something, (3) to contrast or compare, and (4) to conclude or summarize.

Your audience has only its eyes and ears to follow your speech. Unless you have mind readers or psychics in the audience, people will be lost or baffled without clear transitions telling them where you're going next.

Conclude your speech with a signal that you are winding up for a smashing close. Some of the best transitions are "In conclusion..." "To conclude..." "As a result..." "To summarize..." and "In closing..."

YOUR OUTLINE IS A FRIENDLY GUIDE

If you have a clearly defined beginning, middle, and ending to your speech, you will know where you're going, how to get there, and when you've arrived. And so will your audience. They'll be with you from start to finish without getting lost along the way. Your outline keeps you from talking too long about one idea, neglecting important ideas, having to conclude before you're finished, or abandoning your speech because time is up or you don't know how to stop. Consider, for example, the outline for an informative presentation on the next page.

If you have a specific length of time to talk, you can estimate how many words your speech can contain. Most of us speak at the rate of approximately 120 to 125 words a minute. Practice your speech to see how to pace your delivery. Practice won't make a performance, but there won't be a performance without practice.

YOUR OPINIONS ARE NOT FACTS

An opinion is nothing more than an idea that has little significance until it is validated by facts.

It's all right to say you had a disastrous vacation because it doesn't have a great deal of significance that will change someone's life. If you say, "I think that new filing clerk should be fired," you'd better have valid reasons to support your opinion if someone asks, "Why? I think she's doing a good job." The fact that you don't like her hairdo, the way she chews gum, or her inappropriate clothes are all your opinions and may not be those of the department head who hired the woman.

Off-the-top-of-the-head and ill-considered remarks that are merely opinions can be catastrophic if they have no basis in fact or truth. If you expect to be considered dependable and trustworthy, learn to support your opinions with verifiable facts.

SAMPLE OUTLINE

Informative Speech

The University of Iowa has announced that enrollment is expected to drop from 28,045 to 26,806 students in the coming academic year. To offset the loss of revenue, an increase in tuition is planned along with other major proposals.

1. There will be no increases in salaries for the faculty.

2. The budget for purchasing library books will be cut.

3. Repairs to buildings will be reduced by $1 million.

Making these adjustments in the budget will help the university to continue offering high-quality education.

ORGANIZING AN ARGUMENTATIVE SPEECH

The hypothetical speech about the Maine vacation is meant to be entertaining. But many speeches are presentations meant to convince an audience, support a cause, or underwrite new policies. They are debatable issues that need serious treatment.

When you're discussing pro-and-con issues, you get into situations where arguments require logical reasoning. You must acknowledge both sides of an issue if you're to be viewed as a responsible, well-informed, and objective speaker.

The basic organization remains the same as for any other type of speech, with one exception: *You are obligated to present both sides of the issue.*

RECOGNIZING YOUR OPPONENT'S POINT OF VIEW

If you declare, "There's no reason why inflation can't be controlled," you may be pulling the pin on a grenade. The fellow you're talking to may be just as positive that runaway inflation can't be controlled. You (as well as inflation) are out of control if you can't justify your opinion with facts.

There are three ways to do this:

1. *Rank your reasons for your opinion.*

2. *Use facts to support it.*

3. *Make a thorough investigation of the subject.*

Your opponent has a right to an opinion and may have good reasons for it, so you must admit and acknowledge them. Here's how: Before you present your reason for believing as you do, acknowledge the opposition with a lead-in such as:

"I know that inflation is difficult to control using our current method of levying taxes to monitor spending, but..."

SAMPLE OUTLINE

Argumentative Speech

When the bond issue comes up for vote, I urge you to vote against razing the 90-year-old hotel to make way for a mini-mall.

1. Although the City Council has suggested building a retirement home on the outskirts of the city, remodeling the hotel would provide much-needed apartments for senior citizens who need downtown locations.

2. I realize some businesspeople want to upgrade the downtown appearance with modern buildings, but restoration of the hotel would preserve the city's historical heritage.

3. Although some parents with small children think a downtown park might provide picnic facilities or playground equipment, as well as child care services while they shop, preservation of the hotel would add tax revenue for the City that is sorely needed to maintain services.

It is for these significant reasons that I urge you to vote against tearing down the elegant old building.

You then continue by presenting the facts, statistics, and authoritative quotations that support your first "because" or reason.

You then proceed with the same acknowledgment of every issue under consideration and exploration. Unless your audience is assured that you are fully knowledgeable on all issues, you will appear uninformed or irresponsible (or worse, ignorant). You will leave yourself open for heckling, criticism, and challenges.

ORGANIZING YOUR THOUGHTS MAKES YOU THINK

Because thinking is hard work, most of us avoid it. Thomas Edison said, "There is no expedient to which a man will not go to avoid the real labor of thinking." What passes for thinking too often is just pushing prejudices around into new positions.

Alfred Korzybski, a scientist of some sixty years ago, said, "There are two ways to slide through life; to believe everything or to doubt everything. Both ways save us from thinking." When you require yourself to be a responsible thinker, you will spot irresponsible thinking in the reasoning of others and be rewarded:

◆ You will be impervious to the charlatan's appeals.

◆ You will be respected as an objective speaker.

Why does organization work? It works for three reasons.

1. It coordinates your material.

2. It controls your ideas.

3. It develops responsible thinking.

WHEN YOU KNOW WHY, YOUR AUDIENCE WILL, TOO

Every speech has a purpose—or should have. Be aware of what it is. If you use the simple four-sentence outline, it will take you from the start to the finish. Three main ideas are enough for the average person to absorb in one speech, which is why they are usually sufficient for most presentations.

Think of your speech as a journey. Know why you're giving it, where you are going with your ideas, how to get to the conclusion, and how to stop when you get there. On any trip you try to prepare for delays, detours, and distractions that can impede your progress. You can prepare for distractions and disturbances on the speaker's platform, too, when you understand how to cope with them and still proceed calmly to your destination.

The simple four-part outline is sufficient to give you the guidelines necessary to get you safely from start to finish with clear and specific transitions to keep your audience informed of any changes or additions you make as you proceed from beginning to end.

When you know why you're making the presentation, your audience will know it, too. And they will not only be satisfied with but also impressed by your competence and effectiveness.

Chapter 3

How to Get Started:

Eight Ways to Do It

"Our plans miscarry because they have no aim. When a man does not know what harbor he is making for, no wind is the right wind."

—Seneca

When you introduce a friend to someone new, you try to establish rapport in the first few seconds, usually by seeking a mutual interest that links the two strangers together.

To establish rapport with your audience, make the first seconds count. *Smile—Smile—Smile!* Wait until some of them, at least, smile back before you say a single word.

HOOK YOUR AUDIENCE

Every effective communicator uses four key words to hook any audience, be it one or one hundred: *Hey—You—See—So.*

When you smile, you're signaling *Hey.*

When you introduce your subject, the audience becomes *You.*

When you deliver your speech, your listeners *See.*

When you draw your conclusion, you arrive at *So.*

Every speech, regardless of length or substance, requires an introduction. It's the first paragraph with a two-pronged hook that (1) leads into your subject and (2) arouses interest.

The thesis sentence (declaration of your purpose) usually comes at the end of the first paragraph and acts as a launching pad for your speech. This statement becomes the purpose for giving the speech and prepares your audience for the reasons (becauses) of why your vacation in Maine was a disaster.

Here are eight dependable and effective introductions from which you can choose those most applicable to your subject, purpose, and audience:

1. Narrow from general to specific.
A topic like your Maine vacation is simple and doesn't need more specificity. But if you say, "Our foreign aid program needs revision," you are coping with a complex problem with many facets.

You can reduce that complexity by narrowing the subject: "We need to take a hard line toward the military hardware we are shipping into the Middle East." Even that may have to be narrowed further depending on how long you intend to speak.

We call this an *inductive* approach that leads from the *deductive* in these ways:

It reduces the depth and breadth of the subject.

It narrows the subject to one idea.

It can be discussed specifically.

2. Establish yourself as an authority on your subject.

If you are unknown to the audience, you will probably be introduced (adequately and well, we hope) by some dignitary who will announce your credentials and ability to speak on the subject. If this isn't enough to gain the confidence and respect you need to put across your ideas, you may need to establish more credibility. If your profession, acumen, education, or experience qualify you to be considered an authority on your subject, don't hesitate to state this explicitly.

Let's say, for example, that you are a real estate broker competent to discuss land use, zoning regulations, loans, transfers, title searches, building codes, etc., and you are asked to speak to the city council. Your expertise would carry more weight than that of some transient who has never owned anything more than a tent and a frying pan. Your comments on adding a new shopping center certainly have more validity than his. Your audience is entitled to hear your qualifications as an authority to help them arrive at an informed conclusion.

3. Use comparison and contrast.

Your goal is to show the superiority of one thing over another. Notice: *Consider only two things* to determine which is better. It's impossible to evaluate every item in the category your subject embraces. For example: you can compare the advantages of the community's junior college over the state university; you can compare cohabitation with marriage; you can contrast the Toyota with the Volkswagen.

If you are discussing the idea of hiring a new secretary for your firm, you might lead into your speech with a thesis sentence: "I believe a person with a two-year secretarial diploma makes a better secretary than one you train on the job." This obligates you to handle the idea of what makes one idea better than another.

4. Use of details.

Specifics are more effective than generalities. Figures and statistics are often convincing, but they are even more so if they're reduced to their smallest common denominator.

Let's say you're going to discuss the insomnia that is affecting the productivity of your company's work force. You know that three or four persons out of a hundred suffer from sleeplessness. Estimate how many people are in your audience and mentally divide that number by three.

You can begin, "A third of you in this room—approximately thirty—suffer from insomnia yourselves. You know how loss of sleep affects your capability the next day. Here are some ideas that doctors have recommended to help with this problem."

A young woman recruiting high school graduates for a secretarial school introduced herself: "One summer I worked on an assembly line. I sat hour after hour watching 120 hands stuff tubes of toothpaste into boxes while 240 eyes stared blankly at nothing and 60 minds were locked into blankness. Working on an assembly line is a boring job. That's why I went to secretarial school and became a paralegal. You can become a qualified and highly paid secretary in a fulfilling job by attending my academy."

5. Quote an authority.

If you aren't one yourself, quote those who are to give validity and support to your introduction. Be sure the authority is recognized as such. To use basketball star Michael Jordan as an expert on corporate law might not be as convincing as an attorney specializing in this field.

Let's assume you are to speak before your service club on the pros and cons of allowing a nuclear power plant to be built in your area. You know the opposition is strong and vocal. No matter which side of the argument you support, don't rely on hearsay reports from the man on the street, a starry-eyed reporter, or a student in a nearby college. Go to the people with verifiable facts. If possible, choose someone who is well-known and respected even though your audience may disagree with his position. At least they will have to listen to his arguments.

6. Use anecdotes.

Vignettes, or slices of life, are complete little insights into human nature. They may or may not be funny. Sometimes they are sad. But you can involve an audience with them. Collect accounts of bizarre, unusual, heart-tugging, laughable or terrifying accounts of behavior. For instance: The 12-year-old would-be pilot who commandeers an airplane and takes off without permission; the ordeals of a collie that spent three years getting from Maine to Texas to find the family he'd lost on a cross-country move; the 80-year-old grandmother making her first plane trip to Russia; the girl who was kidnapped and held captive for ten days. All such happenings have clout because they are usually true and unusual. They can lend color, interest, and specificity if you relate them to your subject and your audience.

To illustrate: Following a traffic accident, the long-promised stop-light at a dangerous corner is under discussion. You are appealing for action. Remind your audience of the six-year-old boy struck down the first day of school by a tourist who hadn't seen the arterial stop sign hidden by overgrown shrubbery. Embellish your account by telling how he suffered a broken leg and thigh, lost a year of school, and may always walk with a limp. This appeal for action will have more influence than all the accident statistics in your state or county that you might quote.

7. Define your terms.

Thousands of new words have been added to our language since World War II, and technology has coined terms unfamiliar to the average person. Inside jargon and terminology bewilder people who don't have specialized knowledge.

It is important to be sure your audience understands the terms needed to discuss your subject. You may have to use a chalkboard or flip chart if a complicated subject—such as the proposed construction of a nuclear power plant—requires specialized terminology.

8. Use examples.

Nothing is as intriguing as "for example..." "for instance..." "that reminds me..." "once upon a time..." or "you'll recall..." Let's say you're reporting on a national convention of automobile dealers looking for incentives to promote business.

You use specific examples of how various dealers are succeeding. "Jack Riley in Salesville set up a carnival on a vacant lot close to his facility with a razzle-dazzle array of rides and sideshows. He said the excitement brought in a lot of prospective buyers who eventually bought cars.

"Another retailer in Dallas had a huge sale with door prizes, a country-western band, and complimentary coffee and cookies. He said the idea was a roaring success and worth every penny it cost in sales and service jobs."

Remember, to have impact, your examples must relate to the audience. People are interested in anything that involves their health, money, relationships, and success.

INTRODUCTIONS ARE IMPORTANT

They are worth your time, thought, and effort. Half the battle is won when you hook your audience and grab its attention with your introduction.

Calling a speech a battle isn't so farfetched—a speech is a battle! You are battling for your listeners' attention when you propose to entertain, inform, convince, or persuade them to do something. You are obligated to make the time they listen to you valuable.

Your audience deserves the best you can give in return for the time and attention it gives. If you give your introduction the attention it deserves, your audience will give you the attention you deserve.

HOW TO GET OFFSTAGE

Many speakers simply abandon their speeches and sit down. Others introduce a new idea that goes nowhere—leaving the audience wondering why they feel cheated, confused, and bewildered.

The smoothest, easiest, and most satisfactory conclusion is to simply wrap up your main points. For example, "Now, you can see why that disreputable cottage, the aggravating neighbors, and the high cost of everything made our vacation in Maine an experience I never want to repeat."

Keep in mind the baseball diamond. When the batter hits a homer and rounds the bases for a score, he doesn't leave the game at third base and head for the showers, or go sit in the bleachers with his wife. He keeps pounding away for home plate, going back to where he started.

Your speech is like that. When you've finished discussing your last "because," you race for home by repeating your thesis sentence and recapping your major "becauses." You leave your audience with a most satisfying and conclusive ending—fastened with a neat and tidy bow.

Chapter 4

Leave the Stage Fright Backstage:

Getting Rid of Anxiety

"I believe anyone can conquer fear by doing the things he fears to do, provided he keeps doing them until he gets a record of successful experiences behind him."

—Eleanor Roosevelt

Stage fright is considered the fear that can turn stalwart men into cringing wimps. One woman says, "It's like an invisible boa constrictor that wraps itself around me up to my brain until I'm so paralyzed I can't speak."

A man moans, "The human brain is a wonderful thing. It starts working the moment you're born and never stops until you stand up to speak in public."

Public speaking isn't something you do standing behind a podium on the speaker's platform. It's what you do every time you say a word outside the walls of your house. If you think of public speaking as public talking, you will conquer half your fear.

MAJOR CAUSE OF STAGE FRIGHT: TOO MUCH CONCERN WITH SELF

When you become self-conscious you lose confidence. Your purpose as the speaker is not to impress your audience with how remarkable you are, but to *communicate* with it. Communication takes place when the ideas from your mind are transferred to the minds of others without getting lost or becoming distorted along the way.

As the speaker, your sole purpose is to talk to your listeners and tell them why you are the speaker. Speeches are given for a variety of purposes, sometimes more than one. As you prepare your material, ask yourself "Why am I giving this speech? What is my purpose?"

1. To inform

2. To entertain

3. To inspire

4. To convince

5. To motivate

6. To teach

You can't talk to an audience if you don't know *why* you're there. Even getting up to say a few words requires you to know *something* about what you intend to say.

Intent solves half the problem of purpose. Purpose solves most of the fear in stage fright.

PICKING UP NEGATIVE FEEDBACK

Losing eye contact with an audience is probably the first step toward losing control. Confident speakers know how to pick up on negative feedback clues and use them to regain control of an audience's attention. Negative feedback clues include glancing at a clock or watch, restless movements, whispering, tugging at clothes, rustling papers or books, and the like.

If you react nervously to these feedback clues, you may lose control and suffer stage fright.

The minute you see a sign of lack of interest coming from anyone, act, don't react.

HOW TO REGAIN CONTROL

Confident speakers don't allow the audience to see any evidence of concern. They use one or more of the following devices:

◆ Move away from the podium.

◆ Walk around the platform.

◆ Speed up or slow down delivery.

◆ Vary the volume and pitch of voice.

◆ Stand still without making a move.

◆ Ask for a show of hands to involve the audience.

◆ Ask someone in the front row a question.

Don't stand glued to the floor behind the podium. Move around when tension begins to take over. Action takes the brakes off the brain and lets it function. If necessary, pace around like a caged lion on a rampage. Do anything to keep the eyes of the audience fastened on you.

Never read a speech! Never pass out materials to be read by the audience. Use posters, chalkboards, flip charts, overhead projectors, and videocassette players if you must for your presentation. However, avoid prolonged loss of eye contact with the audience. If you need to regain eye contact or refocus attention on you, go to extremes if you have to:

◆ Drop a book or briefcase.

◆ Take a drink of water.

◆ Break a piece of chalk or a pencil.

◆ Leave the platform and walk around the room.

◆ Open or close a window.

Of course, you need confidence to take such drastic actions, but you'll find it reinforced by the startled attention you'll receive from a suddenly wide awake audience wondering what you'll do next. You may feel silly, histrionic, pathetic, or uncoordinated. But you'll regain attention and control.

YOUR STAGE FRIGHT SCARES YOUR AUDIENCE

A nervous, tensed, timid speaker creates a nervous, tensed, fearful audience. If they aren't there as captives, some of them may ignore you entirely. They may fall asleep, read a book, or even leave. You don't want to find yourself facing an audience made up of such timid souls that they're afraid to leave.

Remember: *Present your ideas from your listeners' point of view.* As long as you keep the feelings, desires, and aspirations of your audience uppermost in your mind, you will be tuned into them— not tuned out. *Connect with people.* Stage fright disappears when you know your audience likes you and you're all operating on the same wavelength.

THINK OF PUBLIC SPEAKING AS PUBLIC TALKING

Instead of agonizing, "I have to make a presentation next week to the Rotary Club about the new waste-disposal plant the city's planning to build," think "Next week, I'll be *talking* to the Rotary Club about an important issue facing our city!"

Rid yourself of the terror that giving a speech can create by substituting the idea that you're simply going to get up and talk to interested people about something they want and need to hear about.

TALK SHOWS AREN'T SPEECH SHOWS

The guests who appear on TV talk shows come to talk, not to make speeches. They treat the situation as though they are visiting with a friend in a living room, talking about mutual interests. If viewers thought they'd be listening to a "speech show," they would pass up the program entirely.

Always remember that most audiences are sympathetic and friendly. They want you to succeed. Unless it's an audience made up of dissenters, the people will be friendly and supportive. They are just as anxious to be spellbound as you are to be spellbinding.

Concern yourself with their feelings and desires, and you can't avoid relating to your audience. As soon as you sense the connectedness that you feel with an attentive audience, you will find stage fright slinking backstage.

Part II

Relating to
Your Audience

Chapter 5

◆

Conversing with Your Audience:

Treating Your Listeners as Friends

"Good manners is the art of making those people easy with whom we converse."

—Jonathan Swift

There's something about a podium that turns people into stiff public speakers who deposit their natural selves on the chair when they leave it to face an audience.

Should there be any difference between being a good speaker and a good conversationalist? No. An audience is made up of people just like the people you meet every day and everywhere. So why shouldn't you talk to them in the same easy way when they're sitting in your audience?

Long-suffering audiences pray that someone will yell "FIRE!" to give them a chance to escape from a dreary and dull speaker. But they are permitted only one response—applause. The hypocrisy flatters the bore into a self-styled howling success and perpetuates the false notion that the stage calls for formality.

A person who wouldn't dream of wearing a tuxedo to a backyard barbecue marches up to the podium in much the same pompous way. Pomposity is inelegant anywhere and everywhere.

I have a friend who's in great demand as a lecturer and guest at parties. I've analyzed what makes this man such a popular speaker and sought-after guest. He relates to his audience as a friend—whether it is twenty or two hundred. He tailors his speech and conversations to the occasion and the audience.

He talks about his trips, popular books, antiques, fishing, dogs, and environmental concerns with spontaneity and enthusiasm. He's as completely natural and unaffected on stage as off. He addresses an audience of one hundred as directly as he speaks to an audience of one.

Good public speakers and sparkling conversationalists understand these six rules.

1. *They know when to talk and when not to.*

2. *They talk about things that interest others.*

3. *They use simple, everyday language.*

4. *They talk without pomposity.*

5. *They gesture naturally.*

6. *They maintain eye contact.*

A SENSE OF TIMING IS IMPORTANT

Good timing can turn a mediocre speaker into a sparkling converser. A famous acting coach once remarked, "In my opinion, nothing is as important on stage as timing. But I can't define it. I guess it's something you're born with. You either have it or you don't."

I believe timing is something you *can* master if you learn to pick up on negative feedback clues and respond to them.

An attentive audience is quiet. You're in trouble if some people exhibit lack of interest by shuffling their feet, wiggling on squeaky chairs, coughing, gazing around, whispering, or looking into a purse. When this happens, step up or slow down your delivery.

> *Timing is simply a matter of relating to your audience and then maintaining that relationship no matter what distractions may disturb the atmosphere.*

You should control your audience as a conductor controls an orchestra, a football captain the team's movements, a sergeant his rookies. They are "on stage" just like platform speakers who must deliver no matter what problems arise to thwart them.

The speech that sounds the most natural may have been revised countless times and practiced in front of a mirror countless more. The most spontaneous speaker is also the most controlled in mastery of himself and his material. He understands the power of timing and uses it to control his audience.

YOU CAN GENERATE STAGE PRESENCE

Platform poise is an elusive essence. Basically, it is the outward expression of the inner self. Personality (the reality of your soul) is an intangible combination of characteristics that either attracts or repels an audience.

Elbert Hubbard, a lawyer and writer who served in the U.S. Senate at the turn of the century, said, "In eloquent speaking it is the manner that wins, not words. Your personality is a combination of your traits, tendencies, disposition, vitality, training, and convictions. You are uniquely yourself—unlike anyone else in this world—and that is what you must project to an audience."

GESTURES

People ask, "What do I do with my hands when I'm giving a speech?" The answer? Simple. Just let them hang on the ends of your wrists until you can't keep them still.

Almost everything written about gestures is inane and senseless. A textbook gesture looks textbookish. Elocution teachers did their students a grave disservice when they taught formalized gestures. "Raise your hand here, lower it there, reach out to the audience, hold your hands over your head." The *only* place a gesture comes from is inside you. Gestures come from:

your heart and soul
your instincts
your interest
your involvement

Even speech coaches try to enforce rules. They say, "Never put your hands in your pockets," "Never pound the podium with your fist," "Never move around on the platform." Absolute nonsense. The most effective gestures sometimes violate every textbook rule.

THERE ARE NO RULES FOR ACTION

Abraham Lincoln stood absolutely still, straight, and quiet. He never touched the podium, made wild gestures, or walked around. In contrast, Theodore Roosevelt was a fiery, vital, and bombastic speaker who used his whole body as an instrument of expression.

If you want to be at ease, be natural. Don't let anyone tell you to move here or there, sit or stand, make or not make gestures.

The speaker who is confident and at ease is natural and at home on the platform. Confidence is the font of charisma and what makes a speaker appealing and admired.

HANDLING DISTRACTIONS

No matter how prepared you are, how at ease you feel, and how responsive your audience appears to be, things can go wrong through no fault of yours. You're not speaking into a tape recorder or an empty room; you are dealing with human beings who can do the most unpredictable things.

If someone gets up and walks out of the room, the entire audience is mesmerized and all eyes follow the disappearing distraction. If someone knocks a briefcase off a table or drops a book onto the floor, everyone's attention is drawn from you to the excitement. If something like this happens, your best recourse is to do nothing. As Oscar Wilde once remarked about a confident speaker, "He knew exactly when to say nothing." You might as well stop talking, stand still, and wait until things settle down. No one will be listening to you, anyway.

People on the platform with you can also draw attention away from you. I once watched a TV program where a prominent senator was addressing Congress. Behind him several dignitaries stole the show. One was reading a letter, another kept dozing off and dropping his head while the man beside him kept poking him to wake up, and another official kept smiling at someone in the audience. I can't remember a word of the speech, because the distractions were more interesting.

After-dinner speakers contend with terrible distractions. People are clinking coffee cups, repairing makeup, going to the restrooms, playing with cutlery, drawing on napkins, and whispering. If you can't get attention by rapping a spoon on your glass, coughing, or talking, just stand quietly until your silence becomes so deafening the audience will be embarrassed and give you its attention.

COMMON DISTRACTIONS

1. Playing with your jacket or blouse buttons

2. Jingling coins in your pocket

3. Tossing hair off your face

4. Putting on or taking off your glasses

5. Tugging at a sleeve or collar

6. Making vocalized pauses ("um," "ah")

7. Waving your hands around without a reason

8. Shuffling your feet

9. Rustling your paper or notes

AVOIDING DISTRACTIONS

Some speakers create their own distractions. I recall a minister whose behavior was so distracting I couldn't remember his sermons. He put glasses on to see his audience and took them off to read his notes. I became so fascinated that instead of listening to him, I began counting the number of times he put on and took off his glasses. I can't tell you what he said, but I *can* tell you how many times he fiddled with his glasses.

Gestures that result from tension or anxiety take control of your material and your effect on the audience. If your actions speak so loudly people can't hear what you say, you should revamp your platform behavior. Get a friend to tell you what it is you do that diverts attention away from your message.

BE YOURSELF

At a convention for realtors, I listened to experts talk about their specialties. All of them were authorities, and most of them were boring. When a rumpled little man with flyaway hair and a wrinkled suit stood up, I thought, "Oh, no. Not another dreary speaker!"

He stood before the room of weary and restless people and waited for them to quit talking, get back into their seats, and give him attention. When they finally did, he went into action.

He broke every rule in the elocution textbooks. He ran around the room, gestured wildly, mangled English grammar, never consulted a note. He never lost our attention, either. He was so excited over his subject—rural land use—he excited realtors who were involved only with urban development. He was the most talked-about speaker at that conference.

I also knew a minister who held his listeners spellbound Sunday after Sunday who did nothing of the sort. He stood still behind the podium and rarely gestured or departed from a quiet and controlled delivery. His sermons were masterpieces of organization and content, and his presentations were masterful. He was a gentle, confident, and calm person during the week and remained the same on Sundays.

Speakers who give speeches are so concerned with speechifying, they don't converse with their audiences. There's no secret in talking to audiences. You look at them, talk to them as you would a friend, and be yourself. If you're emotional and expressive off stage, be that way on. If you're quiet and controlled, stay that way when you're conversing with an audience.

When you are the speaker anywhere, for any reason, you have been chosen because of who and what you are. You are qualified to make the presentation or deliver the speech or you wouldn't be doing it.

Always be yourself. Talk to your audience in a natural, easy, and friendly way, and you'll be the charismatic speaker you want to be.

FOUR STEPS TO STAGE STARDOM

1. Never say, "I'm going to give a speech." Say, "I'm going to get up there and *talk* to my audience."

2. Leave textbookish pedantry, patronizing airs, self-interest concerns, and oratorical demagogery on the chair.

3. Treat your audience as guests who've consented to give you some of their precious time and attention. Don't abuse their gift by making them feel like captives who are compelled to listen to you.

4. Converse with your listeners as you would with a friend at lunch, and leave them wishing you would keep doing more of it.

Chapter 6

How to Keep an Audience Awake:

Finding the Ties that Bind

*"You'll never move others, heart to heart,
unless you speak from the heart."*

—Goethe

I laughed at a cartoon with the caption, "And now, in conclusion—
EVERYBODY WAKE UP!" that pictured an after-dinner speaker
addressing a sound asleep audience. Anyone who has sat on a hard
chair in a crowded room listening to a dull speaker who drones on
and on, little knowing (or caring) how dull he is, can relate to that
cartoon.

When such a speaker finally sits down, the polite spattering of
applause falls like manna from heaven, leaving him smug and satisfied. Unconcerned that most of his audience was asleep with eyes
open, he considers himself a spellbinder.

If you want to keep your audience awake, keep them awake. How do you do that? *Talk about what interests people the most: themselves.*

GIVE PEOPLE WHAT THEY WANT

John M. Siddall adopted the policy of giving people what they want when he took over the *American Magazine* in 1915. When he became the editor, the magazine was failing. Siddall established an "Interesting People" department that profiled outstanding people, and increased the circulation by giving people what they wanted. Siddall said, "People are selfish. They are interested chiefly in themselves. They want to know how to get ahead, how to draw more salary, how to keep healthy." When he gave the subscribers what they wanted, he made the magazine one of the most profitable periodicals of the time and it flourished until the 1950s.

People are fascinated by rags-to-riches stories, reports of people who've pulled themselves up by their bootstraps, who have faced and conquered challenges. People won't be sleeping in your audience if you tell them *how* to improve their lives, their bank accounts, their children, their community, their schools, and most of all—themselves.

REINFORCE—REINFORCE—REINFORCE

Actor Will Rogers knew how to captivate audiences. His advice was, "Tell 'em what you're gonna tell 'em, then tell 'em, and then tell 'em what you jes' told 'em you were gonna tell 'em."

The philosophy works because it provides a sense of security and "I've been here before." It's a feeling similar to *déja vu* where a long-forgotten memory is revived.

We're not talking about vocalized pauses such as "you know," "well, anyway," "uuummm," or "like I said." These are meaningless fillers used to provide a sound to keep an audience alert. Unfortunately, they fail. As they become stronger than the message itself, they annoy and distract an audience.

A friend who is a sought-after lecturer on the power of positive thinking uses the same material over and over. I asked, "When you talk on the same thing to the same audiences year after year, don't they get bored?"

He laughed. "Never! They pay to hear me tell them what I've told them before. They feel secure and relaxed knowing what I'm going to say will reinforce what they already believe. It's the same security a child experiences hearing a bedtime story he knows by heart read to him by someone he loves. The familiar is always comforting."

ESTABLISHING AUDIENCE IDENTIFICATION

Before you organize your material and determine what kind of impact you intend to have, ask yourself:

◆ Do the people know and like me?

◆ What is their attitude toward the subject?

◆ Will they be antagonistic or receptive to it?

◆ How much about the subject do they already know?

◆ What is the purpose of my speech?

Audiences vary in size, age, gender, and education. Will you be talking to a men's service club, a school board, the city council, your office associates, a women's church group, the PTA? I don't necessarily mean that you will tailor your talk to suit the audience, but you may be required to be more attentive to your purpose. If you know people will be receptive to you and your ideas, you will be able to take a different approach than if they are resistant or antagonistic.

ANALYZE THE PURPOSE OF THE SPEECH

Every speech is given for a reason. Ask yourself:

1. Why have I been chosen to speak?

2. What is the purpose of my speech?

- ♦ to inform
- ♦ to entertain
- ♦ to persuade
- ♦ to educate
- ♦ to shock

3. Will the audience be antagonistic or receptive?

Where, when, why, what, and who are questions you need to answer before you begin organizing your material, even, if you have a choice, before you choose your subject.

RELATE TO THE HUMANNESS IN US ALL

It's our humanness that links us to one another. We share many emotions, fears, superstitions, regrets, and expectations. We laugh at comedians making fools of themselves. We're smug when someone confesses some dumb thing he did, knowing we'd never be *that* dumb. We cry at funerals because we feel compassion. We suffer over abused children or animals. We empathize with parents who lose children through death.

An audience perks up when the speaker says, "That reminds me of the time..." or "I remember when I was in college..." or "Like your mother, mine always advised..."

You don't have to bare your own soul to an audience; your file of human-interest stories should include a variety you can draw on when you need an example to add color or drama to your material. Your audience will stay awake if you tell them how to make their lives happier, healthier, richer, and friendlier.

BE INTERESTED TO BE INTERESTING

If you are asked to speak on a subject that doesn't excite or interest you, get excited and interested—or stay home. If you can't get excited about a subject, how can you expect to get an audience excited?

Washburn Child, an American ambassador to Italy in the 1920s, once confided the secret of his success as a diplomat. "I am so excited about life, I can't keep still. I just *have* to tell people about it."

That's the kind of excitement that makes you exciting and excites your audience. Excited people won't fall asleep.

FIVE WAYS TO KEEP YOUR AUDIENCE AWAKE

1. Reinforce familiar ideas.

2. Link personal experiences to those of your listeners.

3. Determine the purpose of your speech and stick to it.

4. Appeal to the humanness that links us together.

5. Tell them what you're going to tell them, then tell them, and then tell them what you just told them.

Heads will be nodding, all right. They'll be nodding in approval and appreciation for what you're telling them that keeps them happily awake.

Chapter 7

It's Not Always a Laughing Matter:

Jokes Do Not a Presentation Make

"There are very few good judges of humor, and they don't agree."

—Josh Billings

A funeral is just about the only place where a speaker isn't trying to be funny. Even meteorologists become comedians while explaining weather maps. It's fine to be funny when something *is* funny. But when unfunny things are treated as funny, it's an error in judgment.

A supposedly intelligent speaker who tries to communicate with a supposedly intelligent audience on a serious subject, but who depends on jokes to keep his listeners attentive, lacks propriety.

WHEN JOKES MAKE YOU A JOKER

Many speakers believe that jokes in a speech will make them a howling success. So they search for, listen for, and ask for jokes. They collect jokes—good, bad, lousy, off-color, untimely. Although someone once said a pun is the lowest form of humor, a joke is really lower because it's easier to come by. Laughing at a joke and telling one to make other people laugh are different things entirely.

This is not to say, however, that jokes can't add lilt and sparkle to a speech when they are appropriate to the subject, the audience, and the occasion.

An appropriate joke should be free of innuendo and double meanings. Raunchy, off-color, sexist, mother-in-law, and ethnic jokes can contaminate an entire speech. The few who might enjoy such jokes aren't worth the resentment the majority of the audience will feel.

Example: The speaker at a Christmas party for our local musicians' union announced that his subject would be the humor that handicapped persons create without trying. He then proceeded to imitate a lame man climbing stairs, a blind person fumbling around furniture, a stutterer asking directions, a mentally retarded child trying to catch a ball. On and on he went, supporting his pantomimes with comments on how a handicapped person's actions were funny.

The titters of polite guests soon died away as shame and embarrassment made people look anywhere but at the speaker. Some of the less intimidated got up and left the room. This speaker was so far out of line that his speech should have been confined to his own home, preferably to himself.

Another example of a misguided speaker was a prominent U.S. senator who addressed a group of men he thought would relate to him better if he strung together off-color and sexist jokes. After his speech, one of the men remarked that he felt sick to his stomach. And a number of his friends said the same thing.

Now this wasn't a group of pious wimps. They were seasoned United States marines.

JOKES MUST BE APPROPRIATE

If you hear a joke that you like and it seems appropriate to use in a speech, then use it. But if you've laughed yourself silly at a joke you heard at a poker game, and you think "That's a terrific joke I have to fit into my next speech somehow," you are using the judgment of a man wearing overalls to a formal wedding or a woman going to a business meeting in short-shorts.

Laughter in your audience doesn't necessarily mean you are another Jay Leno. Some of the laughter may be simply kind and

polite. What seems funny to you may strike a nerve in someone else that makes your funny story very unfunny indeed.

A joke should be fresh as a newly minted penny and as new as a just-laid egg. Or it will lay one of its own.

Telling a joke is an art. The timing has to be perfect and the punch line an unexpected delight. Nothing is as unnerving to both a speaker and an audience as to be expecting to hear a smashing climax to a long joke and find it smashing, all right—only because it smashed with a clumsy and unfunny ending.

RACONTEURS ARE FEW AND RARE

Some speakers embrace the idea that a speech should begin with a joke, have several sprinkled throughout, and then end with a clinching joke. They worry about this because they know they're not witty or clever folk.

My advice? You don't have to be a comedian to give a good speech. In fact, you're better off avoiding jokes if you can't tell them well. People blessed with joke-telling skills can get laughs from an audience without effort. But if you're not a naturally funny person, forget the jokes and concentrate on anecdotes that have as much (perhaps even more) impact as jokes.

Too many jokes in a speech make an audience nervous and uneasy. If the speaker is treating a serious subject as a big joke, the listeners suspect flippancy or worse yet, ignorance. There's rarely an occasion when speakers can joke their way through a speech unless they are guest speakers or the master of ceremonies at a roast.

STORIES OFTEN APPEAL MORE THAN JOKES

Anecdotes are little slices of real life—vignettes—that relate to the humanness in us all. They can be sad, happy, tender, heart-breaking, heart-warming, nostalgic, or tear-jerking. The emotions they arouse can involve your audience far more than a joke inserted in order to hear a few chuckles.

Human interest stories have impact. They appeal to your pride, sympathy, fears, likes and dislikes, and compassion for suffering. Collect articles that report kindness to helpless people or animals, injustices to the downtrodden, neighborliness when tragedy strikes, compassion for the underdog, bravery under fire, courage in hazardous situations.

Lace your speech together with fresh, original, and true stories when you need "for instance" remarks. Tailor your anecdotes to the audience and occasion, so they relate to familiar backgrounds, interests, and cultural and educational backgrounds.

Speeches are given for many reasons, and many of them are serious and important. Decide on your purpose. Is it to motivate, entertain, influence voting, support policies, or adopt new guidelines? As a rule, a ratio of three anecdotes to one joke is pushing the humor to the limit in most presentations. Witty asides, clever references, amusing insights, and in-house jokes can keep your audience in a happy mood.

But the best jokes—even told with skill and finesse—do not a presentation make. If you must use a joke, the following tips will help you:

FIVE WAYS TO TELL A JOKE SUCCESSFULLY

1. Tell only the jokes that YOU like.
Even if the joke fits the occasion, don't use it if you don't like the subject or treatment. How can you make it funny if you don't think it's funny?

2. Consider joke selection a serious business.
Make your choice carefully and thoughtfully. If you really need special jokes, consult *Joey Adams' Joke Diary* or Robert Orden's two books, *2500 Jokes to Start 'em Laughing* and *2000 Jokes for Speakers* (Ad-Libbers Handbook). *A Treasury of Humorous Quotations* by Herbert V. Prochnow and his son has more than 6,000 witty sayings suitable for most occasions.

3. Develop your own style.
Study how Tim Allen, Jay Leno, Jerry Seinfeld, and other pros handle their jokes. Each has a different style of delivery that is a trademark. What works for them, however, may not work for you. Find your own style, whether it be snappy one-liners, political, or satire. Sometimes putting yourself into the joke as though you were the object makes it even funnier.

4. Never be offensive.

If you get a laugh at someone's expense, shame on you. Belittling someone for the sake of a laugh comes off as insensitive and cruel, no matter who's telling the joke. An off-color or bawdy joke may get by in some places, but certainly not on the speaker's platform or before a mixed audience. You can make an unforgivable error in judgment that will be remembered long after your presentation is forgotten. Laurence Sterne wrote in *Tristram Shandy* (1760), "For every ten jokes, thou has got an hundred enemies."

5. Select jokes seriously.

Jokes may be funny, but selecting them isn't. Check every joke you intend to use against this list:

◆ Is it appropriate?

◆ Is it in good taste?

◆ Is it necessary?

◆ Is it fresh and sparkling?

◆ Is it harmful to anyone?

◆ Is it one I can tell gracefully?

One last admonition: *When in doubt, leave it out!*

Humor is intangible. It's as elusive as a drop of mercury and as fragile as a whiff of perfume. The saddest thing on the platform is the self-styled humorist who thinks he's funny but isn't. Many things aren't a laughing matter, so don't try to make them laughable by using jokes.

Chapter 8

Getting People to Follow You:

Leaders Know How to Lead

"The question, 'Who should be the boss?' is like asking, 'Who should be the tenor in the quartet?' Obviously, the man who can sing tenor."

—Henry Ford

Among the obligations that may come your way in the course of your personal or professional life is the leadership of a team that is pursuing a particular project or goal. This sort of responsibility may be thrust upon you, you may volunteer for it, or you may assume it by asserting your own leadership expertise. While this kind of assignment may not necessarily involve making formal presentations, the talents required for chairing such a group are similar to and closely related to the skills and poise that are essential for most public speaking.

In every group, someone has to be the leader. Some people collect followers like the Pied Piper. Others straggle and stumble along, tagging after anyone who becomes the leader.

Strangely enough, only one person out of four wants to be a leader. You want to be a leader or you wouldn't be wanting to learn how to lead. Leaders are not born, they are made. Not all people want to be leaders, because it's a lot easier and less demanding to follow a forceful person who is willing to assume the responsibilities leadership requires. Then when things go wrong in the rank and file, the followers can shift the blame to the leader.

WHERE DOES THE LEAD IN LEADERSHIP COME FROM?

Eric Hoffer defines a leader as someone who is "practical and a realist, yet must talk the language of the idealist."

Jack Taylor, a management-development specialist, sees a leader as someone with five qualifications:

1. imagination and above-average intelligence

2. broad interests and abilities

3. skill in oral and written communication

4. adeptness at social interaction with keen insight into human nature

5. sufficient administrative ability to handle projects from start to finish

In writing on management, specialist Edward C. Schleh said, "A leader is a catalyst, one who stimulates others to action, the center from whom others gather strength, the core around which overall cooperation develops."

Alfred J. Marrow, another developer of management skills, emphasizes the humanness of leadership: "True leadership is characterized not by domination but by service. It's a skill involved in the process of two-way communication—a continuous feedback."

THE LEADER'S ROLE IN MANAGEMENT

First and foremost: *An effective leader must be an effective communicator.* You must be able to transfer your ideas without distortion or loss to other minds, so all of you understand the process. Ideas are abstract; they must be handled in a different manner than objects, which are concrete.

For example, if I describe how an apple feels, smells, looks, and tastes to a friend who has never seen an apple, and she goes to market and picks out an apple, I have succeeded in communicating the image of an apple to her mind. If, however, she comes back with an orange or a grapefruit, then I have failed to communicate effectively.

To be a leader with charisma, clout, and courage, you need to observe four directives:

1. Understand the needs and desires of your followers.

2. Consider each one a member of a team, and treat each with respect and consideration.

3. Make each team member feel vital to the cause.

4. Make directives clear, so no misunderstandings occur.

If you fail in any of these four areas, you will find yourself leading a parade with no one in it but you.

THE SECRET OF LEADERSHIP

You can't *command* followers to follow (unless you're an officer in the military). You must *persuade* them by generating the desire to be a member of the team striving to reach a common goal. All members must be made to feel that without each of them, the touchdown will never be made.

President Dwight D. Eisenhower described leadership as "the ability to decide what is to be done and then to get others to want to do it." Good leaders are cheerleaders who inspire enthusiasm and cooperation. At the same time, they must have above-average intelligence but know how to handle it. If they fail to recognize that the majority of followers fall into the "average" category and lose touch with them by talking over their heads or down to them, failure as a leader will result.

Every club, team, scout troop, organization, association, and business needs a leader who can focus attention on a goal and then inspire the members to work toward and achieve it. Every leader has to contend with whiners, foot-draggers, devil's advocates, hecklers, rebels, or absentees. It requires a visionary idealist as well as a down-to-earth realist to meld an unwieldly group into a cohesive team working to reach a mutually agreed-upon goal.

If you can perform in such an enviable capacity, you will become invaluable to your business or association.

HOW YOU COLLECT YOUR FOLLOWERS

Leaders *must* know how to communicate! They have to handle both verbal and nonverbal language to inspire and motivate team members to pull together until the goal is reached. You must win loyalty and cooperation by convincing the team members that the cause demands their allegiance.

The Victorian satirist Samuel Butler wrote "He that complies against his will is of his own opinion still." If you're going to lead, every member of the team must want to be led. Every effort must be wholehearted if you and your followers are to reach the goal.

The communication process includes listening as well as speaking and writing. So a good leader listens to the advice, suggestions, complaints, and experiences of the followers, and then takes them all under advisement.

LEADERS CAN BE DANGEROUS

Persuasive and powerful leaders like Hitler, Mussolini, Castro, Stalin, Lenin, and Napoleon were eloquent speakers who gathered hordes of faithful and adoring followers. They were charismatic leaders, but they were self-serving and lacked the vital quality that makes leaders humane: love for their fellow man and respect for humanness.

Such dangerous leaders gather followers who blindly follow them down the garden path only to find it doesn't lead to the pot of gold but to broken promises and shattered dreams.

There are two sides of the leadership coin. Misguided attachment to the wrong leader can be just as compelling as loyalty to the right one. Sometimes the glitter and glamor that mask demagoguery are far more enticing than truth and reality.

YOUR OBLIGATION

As a leader, you have the power that obligates you to lead your followers in the right direction, for the right purpose, toward the right goal, for the right reasons.

Are you going to lay down the law? Are you going to use your authority to promote yourself or your causes? Are you cloaking selfish intentions with false promises?

If you are charged with leading your fellow workers or associates to a defined and worthwhile goal, you have to inspire your team to follow you—willingly, happily, and purposefully. You can't order them to cooperate; you have to inspire them to. You need to do four things:

1. Design a program that will achieve your goal.

2. Gain the trust and loyalty of your followers.

3. Inspire their confidence in your objectives.

4. Make each team member feel important and valuable.

ESSENTIAL QUALITIES OF LEADERSHIP

Before you undertake the important and critical job of leader, you need to understand and accept seven concepts:

1. Time.

However long you estimate it will take to get the job done, *double it*. Don't undertake your duties expecting to handle them in your spare time. Don't let someone influence you by saying, "Oh, you won't have to spend much time on the job. It's really not that much work to be president (or chairman, monitor, coordinator, or whatever)." Don't let someone throw stardust in your eyes or blind you with glowing promises that can't be fulfilled. Leaders must expect and accept demands and responsibilities.

2. Communication.

Is your job flexible enough so that you can take time to make phone calls, set up appointments with committees, talk with unexpected visitors needing advice? How tolerant are your boss and coworkers about your taking time off for meetings, long lunches, and the like? Do you have access to the word processors and copying and fax machines you will need?

3. Management ability.

Ask yourself, "Can I handle this without losing my temper or letting my prejudices affect my work? Can I give up free time without grousing about it? Am I capable of delegating responsibility and allowing others to assume important jobs without my supervision? Has my experience qualified me for this important job?"

4. Positive family attitudes.

If your leadership requirements demand a lot of time and attention, your family must be supportive and cooperative. You can lose your effectiveness if you believe your family is being neglected because of the time and effort you're expending on the project. A family sometimes has to take a back seat when a parent accepts the demands of leadership. If it can't or won't, your job will be much more difficult and demanding.

5. Patience.

Can you motivate your team to ride out the storms without quitting or undermining your authority? Can you be patient with the uneasy, timid, doubtful, and cantankerous members who may demonstrate personality traits you never suspected they had?

6. Flexibility.

Can you roll with the punches, cope with dissenters, and handle emergencies without coming unglued? You may have to explore new avenues, make unexpected detours, repair breakdowns in relationships, and readjust your timetable for the completion of the project.

7. Stamina.

Can you toss and turn through restless nights and still get up cheerful and go whistling off to another demanding day at the office?

Finally, how would you answer this question:

> *If everybody followed you*
> *Completely to the letter*
> *Tell me, if they followed you*
> *Would the world be any better?*

If the answer is "yes" to all of these questions, you are a treasure who is not only prized by your company but by your fortunate followers.

Chapter 9

Making Meetings Meaningful:

You're the Producer, Director, and Star

"A leader is best when people barely know he exists. When his work is done, his aim fulfilled, they will say, 'We did it all ourselves.'"

—Chinese Proverb

Sooner or later, you are going to be in charge of a meeting. You may not realize that more than eleven million meetings are held every day in the United States. You will probably sit through more than 9,000 hours of meetings during your lifetime. That means more than 365 days of sitting on hard chairs in meeting rooms.

In the world of commerce, time is money. When you are at a meeting, your company is not only losing the time you are away from the office, but dollars as well. Do you have any idea how much it costs your company for you to attend a meeting? Worse yet, how many meetings have you suffered through that weren't worth the time, money, and effort put into them?

The meeting will be worth all this if it is helpful, well organized, well conducted, and focused. Unfortunately, far too many meetings are a waste of time as well as money.

Sooner or later, someone's going to put a gavel in your hand and say, "You're in charge." How prepared will you be to make your meeting productive, worthwhile, and rewarding?

The first rule: *Never call a meeting unless you have a reason.* People are "meetinged" to death. They're disgusted with the wasted effort most meetings create. Often people who want to feel important call a meeting to impress others. Most of what is accomplished at many meetings could be done by phone, office communiques, or through personal discussions.

SEVEN PRELIMINARY STEPS TO A SUCCESSFUL MEETING

Let's say the meeting you are to produce and conduct *is* important. Here is how you go about planning, handling, and controlling a meeting that will be gratifying to the attendees and be worth the time and money spent putting the affair together.

STEP 1

Know why the meeting is being held

Is this meeting taking place:

◆ to focus on a specific problem?

◆ to propose new policies or procedures?

◆ to explain new plans?

◆ to conduct a workshop for an exchange of ideas?

◆ to discuss the hiring and firing of an employee?

◆ to teach new office equipment?

STEP 2
Decide who should attend the meeting

Don't invite anyone who can't contribute something worthwhile. A rule known as Shannan's Law says the length of the meeting rises with the square of the number of persons in attendance. Anyone who doesn't have a real reason to be there can be disruptive, irritable, bored, and resentful.

Try to limit attendance to those who know what's going on and who will be supportive and cooperative. If you have to include people who might be argumentative, fortify yourself with enough people who have the welfare of the company or organization at heart. If you know you will be confronted with dissenters, foot-draggers, and diehards, be prepared to deal with them in a confident and positive way.

STEP 3
Choose the meeting room with care

You may not have a choice, but if you do, choose a place with amenities and conveniences that provide the basics. These include:

◆ good ventilation

◆ adequate and comfortable chairs

◆ tables for books, briefcases, and coats

◆ enough chairs for reporters, unexpected guests, or monitors

◆ a public-address system that works

◆ any chalkboards, flip charts, overhead projector, extension cords, or VCR that may be required

◆ speaker's stand, pitchers, water glasses, and perhaps ashtrays

STEP 4
Announce details in advance

Spell out the *where*, *when*, *why*, *what*, and *who* so everyone who'll be attending knows where to go, why they're going, and what they can expect to do when they get there.

STEP 5
Understand the laws governing open and closed meetings

If you belong to a private corporation where all funds are controlled by management, you may be able to schedule major policy setting meetings without informing the media or the public.

Any meeting, however, that involves the distribution of tax money *must* be open to the public—wanted or not. City council meetings, school or library board meetings, art or literary organizations funded with tax dollars and similar public groups must invite the general public, the media, and any interested persons to attend.

The laws governing open and closed meetings may be strictly enforced. You are responsible for getting announcements into the media far enough in advance so anyone who wants or needs to attend can plan to do so.

Breaches of regulations concerning open and closed meetings can be punished severely. Get the rules for conducting open meetings from your state legislator, so you won't inadvertently violate any of them.

STEP 6
Prepare for interruptions

Some people are late for everything. Ignore them. Provide empty chairs by the door so latecomers won't be disruptive trying to find a vacant seat. Start on time even without a quorum, for a lot of business can be transacted without voting on motions. Speak privately to foot-draggers about getting to your meetings on time, and make sure they realize how important promptness is for the success of a meeting.

STEP 7
Show rather than tell

Most people see better than they hear. Use plenty of visual aids if your presentation requires specific facts or numbers. However, you should try to avoid passing out papers or reports during the meeting. The minute people get them, their heads duck and they start reading—and you lose vital eye contact. If it's absolutely necessary that reports must be read before discussing, then set a time limit and sit down and read along with the others. You may just as well, because nobody will pay any attention to what you're saying or doing while they read the papers. Wait until the end of the meeting to distribute reports for future reference.

DIRECTING THE MEETING

1. Lay down ground rules.
Explain time limits on discussion, scheduled breaks (when and how long), designated smoking areas (if permitted), and other logistics.

2. Give everyone a chance to speak.
You don't want to be accused of favoritism or ignoring people you don't want to hear, but you do need to keep arguments from flaring into disagreeable debates. Depend on your supporters as much as possible and try to keep dissenters from usurping the floor.

3. Encourage quiet persons to contribute.
Sometimes the most retiring and self-effacing person has the most to offer. If you have such people present, arrange for them to sit near you. Something about sitting next to the chairperson or president encourages timid people to speak up.

4. Keep Mr. and Ms. Know-it-all from dominating the meeting.
Even if the person is qualified, informed, and important, don't let a disruptive and aggressive person dominate the meeting. If possible, try to assign him or her a seat in the back so you can ignore a waved hand or other bids for attention. Better yet, give that person something to do to keep busy—keeping notes or handling the props, for example.

5. Keep your eye on the clock.
Assign a time limit to every item on your agenda and maintain it. If things get heated and the discussion threatens to run away with your schedule, then appoint an *ad hoc* committee to study the particular item and report back on it at a later date.

6. Control distractions.

Outside noises are hard to control. But keep whisperers attentive by calling on them for comments or for answers to questions. If others shuffle papers or books so much that they become a nuisance, ask them to desist and settle down. Stop talking altogether if you can't keep people quiet. Your silence becomes so obvious everyone quiets down wondering what is happening. If none of these ploys work, you may have to simply tell the disrupters to quiet down. If this is a habitual distraction that annoys both you and the other attendees, talk to the offenders after the meeting.

7. End the meeting on a high note.

Thank everyone for coming; express appreciation for their contributions; praise them on what's been accomplished. Everyone sacrifices something to attend a meeting and likes to feel it's been appreciated. You can always find something constructive to say about what's taken place. Make everyone feel a part of the action.

WHAT TO DO AFTER THE MEETING

Send a written report to those who should have been there but weren't. Keep a copy of your letter attached to the agenda and file them away for future reference. As the leader, it is your responsibility to see that every agenda for every meeting is filed in chronological order.

It's assumed leaders understand parliamentary procedure, but if you don't, get a made-easy aid such as *Roberts Rules of Order* that will show at a glance how to use rules for making and passing motions, handling discussion, and all the other formal points of order.

SAMPLE AGENDA

Order of Business

1. CALL TO ORDER.

2. READING OF MINUTES. Call for additions or corrections. If none, ask for motion to approve.

3. COMMUNICATIONS. Secretary reads correspondence.

4. REPORTS.
    a. President (or chairperson)
    b. Vice president or vice-chairperson
    c. Recording secretary
    d. Treasurer
    e. Standing or *ad hoc* committees

5. UNFINISHED BUSINESS.

6. NEW BUSINESS.

7. ANNOUNCEMENTS.

8. PROGRAM/SPEAKER.

9. ADJOURNMENT.

TYPES OF MOTIONS

1. Main motion: Only one motion can be pending at any one time.

2. Subsidiary motion: Can be made while main motion is pending, but only if it pertains to the main motion under advisement.

3. Incidental motion: May be a temporary interruption if directly related to main motion.

4. Privileged motion: If important enough to interrupt the discussion and has a direct bearing on main motion, it can be considered.

These standard procedures are from Roberts Rules of Order. *If rigid formality is required for your meetings, follow parliamentary procedure with care and caution. Get a simple manual to keep you from making errors that could be costly, embarrassing, or culpable.*

◆

Part III

Becoming a
Confident Speaker

Chapter 10

Overcoming Inferiority:

Facing Up to the Four P's

"Remember, no one can make you feel inferior without your consent."

—Eleanor Roosevelt

Being defeated by the "Four P's" keeps many a potential spellbinder sitting in an audience instead of speaking to one. Unless you're confronted with rowdies, hecklers, and enemies, your audience not only wants you to perform with elegance and style but will help you do it by being attentive and receptive. You can speak with confidence if you refuse to allow the Four P's to rule your life:

◆ *Passing the buck*

◆ *Pessimism*

◆ *Procrastination*

◆ *Personal Appearance*

ONE
Passing the Buck

Did your parents tell you that "children should be seen and not heard?" Were you afraid to speak up because it wasn't nice to expect grown-ups to listen to you? Early conditioning by critical or overly conscientious parents may have intimidated you. You may hesitate to open your mouth for fear the words tumbling out will be inappropriate, ill-advised, or even unwanted. You can overcome this childhood fear if you know how.

1. *Recognize* it as the childhood fear it is. Refuse to give it power over your adult behavior.

2. *Understand* that this form of stage fright is caused by "purpose tremor." This term is applied to the paralyzing fear that unnerves someone trying too hard to succeed. Banish this fear by thinking, "I wouldn't be asked to express my ideas or get up and talk if people didn't think I could."

3. *Ignore* your bothersome conscience. It's a childish hangover that you'll be scolded for speaking your mind.

4. *Reprogram* yourself by substituting "right" for "wrong" when you are debating whether to speak up.

You will have to stop passing the buck if you're going to overcome a fear of speaking attributed to childhood conditioning.

TWO
Pessimism

So you flubbed a speech once in high school, and now you hold onto that memory. So what? Do you think captivating communicators started delivering spellbinding speeches in their playpens? If all polished and poised speakers gave up before they got that way, we would have many vacant auditoriums instead of hundreds of speakers on platforms.

Eleanor Roosevelt, admired around the world for her ability to captivate audiences of every kind, was terrified when she first began speaking. She said, "I believe anyone can conquer fear by doing the things he fears to do, providing he keeps doing them until he sets a record of successful experiences behind him."

Pessimism is a state of mind—an attitude—a habit. If you're not a born optimist, you can train yourself to be one. Marcus Aurelius said, "A man's life is what his thoughts make of it," and William James concurred: "Human beings can alter their lives by altering their attitudes of mind." Here are four ways to overcome pessimism:

1. *Count the number of negatives you use in a day.* How often do you say, "I can never finish on time," "I don't want to," "I can't get started," "I don't know how," or "I can't prepare a speech for that seminar"?

2. *Rid your mind of pessimistic thoughts.* Two thoughts cannot occupy the same space at the same time. You have to shove out the "I-can't" thoughts and substitute them with "I-can" beliefs.

3. *Become a master, not a slave.* Ben Sweetland wrote in *I Will:* "I was so timid I couldn't talk to three people at one time without becoming tongue-tied. I was a hand-wringer until I read Lincoln's *Proclamation of Emancipation.* Then I decided I would no longer be a slave to my timidity."

4. *Think of your audience as a mirror.* If you scowl at it, it will scowl back. If you smile, it smiles. An audience is made up of individuals, so talk to an audience as you would to one of those persons—a friend. If you were afraid to speak to your friends, you wouldn't have many. If you snarled and scowled at your colleagues and associates, you would find yourself left alone. Your audience reflects you. They come to listen to you, even if they are required to be there. So act happy to see them and they will look happy to see you.

THREE
Procrastination

If idle hands are the devil's workshop, then procrastination is the devil's playground. Procrastinators like to think of themselves as being able to resist pressure, appeals, demands, entreaties, or commands. Outwardly, they appear in control of themselves. Inwardly, they are scared-to-death little kids afraid of failure. They put off trying in order to avoid failing.

Procrastination will destroy your potential, keep you from getting where you want to, and deprive you of life's rewards and satisfactions. And here are four ways to stop procrastinating:

1. *Reinforce desire with action.* Force yourself to act even when you're afraid to act. Never allow an opportunity to "stand up and say a few words" pass you by. Create the opportunities if they don't just happen along.

2. *Seize the moment.* Every moment that passes is gone forever. Follow thought with action. Set up new directives to your brain that demand participation, action, and involvement. Every chance that presents itself for you to speak up, grab it.

3. *Express yourself.* Poised and confident speakers never put their emotions or ideas on hold even though they may be strictly monitoring them. Don't allow your emotions to simmer down, because they will evaporate and lose the fire and fervor that give you charisma and individuality.

4. *Do it today.* Procrastinators say, "Never do today what you can put off until tomorrow." You have to learn to say, "Never put off until tomorrow what I can do today." You must become heroic and aggressive by creating chances to speak if they don't happen inadvertently. Offer yourself as a speaker, chairperson, or monitor every chance you get.

FOUR
Personal Appearance

Ninety percent of us are dissatisfied with the way we look. This includes beauty-pageant winners, fashion models, movie stars, and sex symbols, as well as you and me. We are so engrossed in concentrating on flaws and defects that we fail to prize the assets we do have. Centering on self makes us self-conscious, self-critical, and self-deprecating.

Imperfections occur everywhere, even in ourselves, but we don't hate the world or ourselves because of them. In our search for approval and acceptance, we try to conform to standards of beauty and change from decade to decade.

William James said, "Act as if you were beautiful, confident, and poised, and you will be." Beauty is in the eye of the beholder, but when the beholders are ourselves, we tend to concentrate on the unbeautiful instead. Consider these five ways to cope with personal appearance:

1. *Concentrate on the positive*—not the negative. Never draw attention to flaws or defects in the way you look, talk, or perform on stage or off. All that does is emphasize the very flaws you want deemphasized.

2. *Become more "you" involved and less "me" involved.* Self-consciousness results from too much conscious attention to self. It's oversensitivity to how you feel, look, and behave that puts you in the forefront and others in the background.

3. *Avoid meaningless movements.* Don't fuss with your hair, clothes, pencils, papers, briefcase, or glasses. Use your hands to emphasize your ideas, not to aimlessly distract from them. Dress appropriately for the occasion and then don't fiddle with your clothes or even think about them. If you can't stop, then draw as little attention to your clothes as possible.

4. *Visualize to actualize.* Create in your mind's eye the image of how you want to look, sound, act, dress, and perform. See yourself as poised, confident, captivating, and appealing. You will create on the outside what you see on the inside. Nothing ever materializes until it is visualized first.

5. *Tap into the "life instinct."* There is a life force that propels, generates, and motivates, creating energy and the will to conquer challenges. Plug into this energizing power—it's there waiting to be used when you demand it. The way you appear, appeal, and attract depends on how you use that God-given potential that is uniquely yours—making you an individual unlike any other in the universe.

You can conquer your fears when you know what they are and then work to banish them. Poised and confident speakers probably have had to conquer the same fears that confront all of us when we're asked (or required) to give a speech. When you stop believing that poised and controlled speakers were born that way, you will quit copping out by saying, "I've always been scared to speak up, and I just know I can't get over that fear."

Speakers who captivate an audience have been challenged by the same doubts and fears as you have, but they conquered them just as you want to—and will do. You may not always be a winner, but you'll never be a loser as long as you keep trying.

SUMMARIZING THE FOUR P's

◆ Quit blaming your parents for your inferiority. Concentrate on what was good about your childhood (there had to be *something*). Quit passing the buck and acting like a child. Grow up.

◆ Optimists aren't born. They become optimists by being optimistic. They make the best of it when they're getting the worst of it. And they don't whine when they are getting the worst of it.

Pessimists see the hole in the doughnut; the optimists eat the doughnut around the hole.

◆ Procrastinators are closet cowards. If you had enough courage to get where you are, you have enough to get where you want to be. So buckle up and buckle down.

◆ There's only one Julia Roberts and Mel Gibson, so don't be jealous because they're gorgeous and you think you aren't. Change what you don't like about yourself and accept what you can't change. As the famous Gypsy Rose Lee said, "You have to accentuate the positive and eliminate the negative." She did it with her fans but you can do it with your eyes. It's a matter of seeing what you want to and not seeing what you don't want to.

Conquer the Four P's by putting them in their place—and that isn't your place.

Chapter 11

◆

Your Voice Reflects Your Personality:

It Can Make or Break Presentations

"There are tones of voice that mean more than words."

—Robert Frost

Words take on different meanings at different times in different situations. Communication takes place in these ways:

- 7 percent through words

- 38 percent through sounds

- 55 percent through body language

If more than one-third of what we're trying to communicate fails or succeeds by the *way* we speak, it behooves all of us to think about how we sound when we talk.

Your voice is more personal than your fingerprints. It reveals your character, moods, attitudes, and emotions. Every time you open your mouth to talk, you are selling yourself, your ideas, your merchandise, your services.

A writer depends on grammar and punctuation to give meaning to the printed word. Here are five principles you can use for oral delivery:

1. *Punctuation*

2. *Projection*

3. *Pitch*

4. *Pace*

5. *Perceptivity*

PRINCIPLE ONE
Punctuation

In speaking, a pause without any filler of sound provides a comma or period. Some speakers are so terrified of a pause or any silence in their delivery, they fill it up with vocalized sounds: "aaa" or "mmm." These sounds can be so distracting the audience listens more to them than to the spoken words.

No matter how long a pause seems to you, it never seems as long to your listeners. Give your listeners a chance to assimilate what you've said and prepare for your next words.

Take a look at this sentence and see how oral punctuation changes the meanings. "Jake said Robert's boss needs a course in public speaking." Perfectly clear? Yes, if that's what Jake really said. Let's put in two commas (indicated by pauses in your speaking) and see what happens. "Jake," said Robert's boss, "needs a course in public speaking." If you were saying this, you would do it like this.

"'Jake' (pause) said Robert's boss (pause) 'needs a course in public speaking.'"

PRINCIPLE TWO
Projection

For this you need energy to control your breathing. You create this by speaking from the diaphragm instead of the throat. Shouting is not projecting. And it is not the way to project your voice for two reasons: it is extremely exhausting and it damages the voice mechanism.

When you breathe from the diaphragm, you increase the breath energy that enables you to project your voice to the back of the room. This control of energy is like having an overdrive on your car to shift into when you're faced with an emergency.

To illustrate: Winston Churchill was addressing a huge audience when the sound system failed. In answer to the cries of "Louder! Louder! We can't hear you!" he grabbed the microphone and threw it on the floor. "Now that we have exhausted the resources of science, let us fall back on Mother Nature," he said.

A strong and vibrant voice such as Churchill's exudes confidence and self-assurance. The person with a small, muffled, whispery voice appears weak and hesitant. The speakers who are unable or unwilling to speak in a clear voice are either lacking in self-confidence or are so indifferent to the audience they don't care if they are heard or not.

PRINCIPLE THREE
Pitch

Pitch adds color, variety, and vibrancy to your voice. The way you pitch your voice either enhances or detracts from your message. Here are four ways an audience can be turned off by the pitch of your voice:

1. *Too high.* If you have to pitch your voice so high you're practically shouting, you intimidate the audience, which may find you threatening and overbearing. It also strains your voice mechanism.

2. *Too low.* If the audience has to strain to hear a soft and feathery voice for any length of time, the effort becomes too much and attention fades away.

3. *Too shrill.* When a person is under stress or suffering from anxiety, the voice may become strained and shrill. There's a tendency to raise the voice higher and higher as the stress rises.

4. *Too strident.* Angry and aggressive people talk louder and more harshly the more agitated they become. If you are ever engaged in

an argument, try lowering your voice. You will discover that "a soft answer turneth away wrath," and as you lower your voice to a more soothing level, the tense situation becomes less so.

PRINCIPLE FOUR
Pace

As the speaker, you are familiar with your material and can move around with ease. Your audience, however, doesn't know what you're going to say, and if you race through your sentences, your listeners will be left behind wondering what has been said. If your subject is complex or unfamiliar to the audience, slow down your delivery. Varying the pace will keep your audience alert. If you drone on and on with the same rate and pitch, you will bore your listeners until they fall asleep—or wish they could.

PRINCIPLE FIVE
Perceptivity

If you are sensitive to your listeners and adjust your actions to their reactions, you will instinctively know what to do to maintain their attention.

YOUR VOICE IS A MIRROR
Your voice reflects the inner you. Your subject may be fascinating, your appearance impressive, and your stage presence professional, but if you drone on and on in a dull, listless voice, or rave and rant in a harsh, loud voice, you will alienate your audience. When an audience is restless, uneasy, nervous, or intimidated by a bombastic speaker, it is tuned out and turned off. If that happens, it's your fault. If you don't vocalize them in the most appealing way, the words you have carefully assembled can fall on deaf ears.

Pindar (533–422 B.C.) wrote in his *Isthmian Ode 4*, "For whatsoever one hath well said goes forth with a voice that never dieth." And Homer wrote in the *Odyssey*, "He ceas'd; but left so pleasing on their ear his voice, that list'ning still they seem'd to hear."

If you have doubts about the color, variety, timbre, and pitch of your voice, ask a trusted friend how your voice affects people. You can improve its quality by listening to yourself on a tape recorder. You may decide you need practice at home or even voice lessons, but don't neglect or minimize the importance of a pleasing and attractive voice.

Practice changing the pitch, pace, strength, and color of your voice. Most people aren't aware of how their voices sound and how revealing the voice can be. You can make what you say mean more if you say it in the best possible way with the most expressive and attractive voice.

UNDERSTANDING YOUR VOICE MECHANISM

Producing sound is a complicated process. Many people believe that the sound produced by one's voice comes from the vocal cords, but the strength and quality of the voice actually comes from more than those delicate and fragile vocal cords. The lungs, lips, teeth, mouth, tongue, and hollow spaces around the forehead are all involved.

DEVELOPING VOICE PROJECTION

You need breath energy to project the voice to the back of a large auditorium as well as to the front row. Breathing through the mouth is not the way to project your voice, because you'll make gasping or snorting sounds if you're using a microphone.

Here's how to develop breath energy:

◆ Sit with your arms resting on the arms of a chair.

◆ Relax your neck, shoulders, and throat.

◆ Start whispering "Aaahhh" and feel the warmth the vowel sound makes.

◆ Take deep breaths from your diaphragm and hold them for as long as you can. Practice this when you're stalled in traffic, reading the paper, watching TV, or waiting for a traffic light.

DEVELOPING VOICE RESONANCE

A melodious, colorful, and expressive voice comes from using the "echo chamber" in your head. (This sound can be compared to singing in the shower.) Here are some exercises for developing a rich, colorful voice:

Take a deep breath through your mouth and hum the "mmm" sound. Do you feel a warm tingling in your lips?

Combine the "mmm" with a vowel: mow, mow, mow—cow, cow, cow—now, now, now. Try to force your breath into the echo chamber by consciously bringing the sound into the front of your mouth.

BRINGING YOUR VOICE UP FRONT

I can remember speech teachers in college saying, "Your voice is in the back of your throat. Bring it forward—Up, up, up." Vowel sounds (a, e, i, o, u, and sometimes y) are formed when the throat is open and relaxed and your voice is coming from just behind the front teeth.

Try this exercise to master this important ability. Say aloud these words: coal, coal, coal, holding one hand in front of your mouth and funneling the sound back into it. Feel how the word sounds coming from behind the lips. Then, let it drop to the back of your throat and note the difference in the quality of your voice. Notice how older people's voices sound tired and worn, which happens when they lose the energy to project the voice from the front of the mouth. Their voices have dropped back into their throats.

MAGNIFYING YOUR VOICE

You don't intensify your voice by shouting, which damages the delicate voice cords. You develop amplification by this kind of exercise:

Take a deep breath (through your mouth) and say, "I will say 'Aaahhh' to that nearby chair. Then I will project my voice and talk to that chair across the room. Then I will talk to the chair in the next room without shouting. I can throw my voice like a ball if I concentrate on doing it."

Practice throwing your voice across the room without shouting or screaming.

LAZY TONGUES MAKE LAZY ENUNCIATION

The tip of your tongue is used to make the l, t, and d sounds. If you don't put the tip of your tongue on the gum above the upper front teeth when you form these sounds, you make what's called a "glottal stop," which is a slurred and sloppy sound.

Howard Garrett, public speaker, suggests you repeat this verse as fast as you can and see how hard your tongue has to work:

> *If to hoot and to toot a Hottentot tot*
> *Were taught by a Hottentot tutor,*
> *Would the tutor get hot if the Hottentot tot*
> *Were to hoot at the Hottentot tutor?*

Whenever you hear slurred enunciation, check to see if the speaker is allowing a lazy tongue to keep his speech from being clear and sharp.

FROZEN LIPS MAKE SLURRED SOUNDS

Some people never move an upper or lower lip. (Watch actors on television whose speech you admire or dislike, and see how much or little they use their lips.)

Mobility of the lips is extremely important for clear and crisp enunciation. To increase flexibility of the lips make the "ooo" sound with your lips formed into a pout. Then stick the end of your thumb in your mouth keeping the tip of your tongue touching the lower gum. The "ooo" sound should come out mooon, mooon, mooon—swooon, swoooon, swoooon—crooon, crooon, crooon. Watch your lips in a mirror and see if both of them are moving.

Then say "Who me?" by pronouncing "Who" through pouted lips, then "me" with the lips drawn back in a wide grin. Repeat this exercise every chance you have to make your lips flexible and mobile.

Your voice is a treasure to be protected, cultivated, and prized. It is one of the most valuable components in communicating effectively. Learn to use it to the best of your ability, and it will serve you well.

LOVELY VOICES REAP LOVELY REWARDS

John Robert Powers of the Powers Modeling School said, "A beautiful woman is like a beautiful necklace; when one link is broken, the whole chain is useless. Speech is a vital link in that beauty chain."

This is why fashion models take voice training even though they may never speak a word on the runway or in fashion shows.

Voice-over celebrity Reed Farrell said, "Silvery voice tones yield golden paychecks." The voices you hear cartoon characters speaking are usually those of people who make substantial incomes without ever appearing in front of a camera.

Treasure your voice as a prized possession. Treat it with love and respect. Use it with pride.

Chapter 12

◆

Attributes You Need to Succeed:

Commit Yourself to the Three C's

"Life was meant to be lived and curiosity must be kept alive."

—Eleanor Roosevelt

Francis Bacon (1561–1626) wrote in *Of Studies*, "Reading maketh a full man, conference a ready man, and writing an exact man." After a man reads, confers, and writes, then he is prepared to speak—and do it with elegance and eloquence.

If you want to become a dynamic communicator, you will have to commit yourself to the three C's:

Curiosity
Courage
Consistency

It takes commitment to these three C's if you're going to rise above mediocrity. With the commitment, you will become a full person willing and able to take your place on any platform and perform with confidence.

FIRST

Curious Folk Learn More

Children are curious little persons with a tiptoe expectancy that makes them constantly ask "Why?" It's a pity they lose that eagerness to pursue the unknown when they become grown-ups. The adult who retains that interest learns what makes people tick and comes to better understand them.

"We coddle our minds until they become lazy," observed Rollo May in *Courage to Create*. "We must continually beat our minds into activity by keeping them crackling with 'what if,' 'why,' and 'supposing.'" Thinking feeds upon thoughts. The more you have to think about, the more you can think. The more you know, the more you want to know.

Words are tools for thinking. There are millions of words in our English language. How many do you know or use? As long as people stay in school, they are forced to increase their vocabulary. During the next twenty-five years, however, their vocabulary changes no more than it did in two years of college study. Develop the courage to continue learning.

Jargon appeals to the curious. It is the glue that binds groups together. The jargonnauts talk a language that sounds foreign to the outsider. How much do you understand the jargon of street gangs, truckers, railroaders, police officers, scuba divers, circus performers, astronauts, or musicians?

To illustrate: If I said, "I've been working on my paradiddles, 7-roll fillers, rim shots, and buzzing," would you know what I had been doing? If I went on, "It's a job to disconnect the Speed King pedal, pack the Zildjians, riding toms, and throne, and get to a gig," would that make any more sense to you?

It wouldn't have made sense to me, either, if I hadn't taken drum lessons. That's the inside language drummers use, which I wouldn't use talking to a philatelist unless she was a drummer, too.

No matter what type of work you do or what kind of people you associate with every day, you understand one another. That is why you communicate with insight and meaning. But what happens when you step outside your arena of activity and meet people who don't understand your in-house jargon? Do they understand you? Maybe. Maybe not.

CASE STUDY

Take Joe, for example. He went to work every day and could barely manage to say "good morning" to his colleagues because he was so timid and felt so uninteresting. At the insistence of a friend, he joined a painting class at the recreation center. To his complete surprise, Joe discovered he had a talent for drawing.

Before long, he was presenting his work in art shows, where he began winning honors and awards. He was beside himself with excitement and newfound confidence. He began talking so much about his newly discovered world and using the jargon he'd learned from his classmates and teacher, he couldn't stop telling everyone about his new life.

Learning anything new helps link you to others and provides insights and understandings that bind people together.

Curiosity opens new frontiers and pushes back horizons. The more you learn, the more you earn—not only in money but in self-assurance, self-approval, and self-appreciation. And that leads to the ability to present yourself in the best possible light whenever you want to communicate.

SECOND
Add Courage to Curiosity

Webster's Dictionary defines courage as "mental or moral strength to venture, persevere, and withstand danger and fear of difficulty."

Writing in *Psycho-Cybernetics* (Wilshire, 1972), Dr. Maxwell Maltz said, "We must have courage to bet on our ideas, to take the calculated risk, and to act. Everyday living requires courage if life is to be effective and bring happiness."

You have courage or you wouldn't be interested in exploring new frontiers, taking on bigger jobs, or facing challenges and overcoming them.

You wonder if spellbinding speakers, who captivate and control audiences like magicians, suffer stage fright. They do. Very few people ever become powerful communicators, on stage or off, without having had to muster the courage to get up and speak when they would rather sit still and listen to someone else.

It takes courage to stand up and talk—sometimes just to sit down and talk. My attorney confided, "I experience stage fright every

111

time I walk into the courtroom. Sometimes just talking to a client scares me to death. Facing a jury was sheer terror until I learned to speak to each juror as an individual and a friend. Listening to myself giving advice or pleading a case gives me stage fright." It might interest you to know this man is a trial lawyer of great stature who rarely loses a case, whose clients consider him a poised, confident adviser.

Listen to what other powerful speakers have said. William Jennings Bryan confessed, "My knees fairly smote together the first time I spoke in public." Mark Twain conceded that the first time he gave a speech his mouth was full of cotton and his pulse was speeding fast enough to win a prize cup. Said David Lloyd George, "The first time I attempted to make a public talk, I was in a state of misery. It is not a figure of speech but literally true that my tongue clove to the roof of my mouth, and at first, I could hardly get a word out." "I would rather have led a cavalry charge than face the House of Commons for the first time," admitted Disraeli.

Courage requires more than wish power. It demands willpower. You need steam to move the engine; you need boiling water to make tea. So you need passion and desire to provide the courage to stand up and speak when you feel inadequate.

Courageous people accept limitations. They realize everyone faces limitations, but they know people need them just as a river needs its banks. Some of our limitations we can control—others we can't. The secret is knowing the difference. Butting your head against a stone wall is not courage, it is foolishness. You have to live within your personal boundaries without submitting to them, without letting them control you instead of you controlling them.

Hang this sign over your mirror and consult it every day:

> *The only chains that will bind me are those I forge myself in fire of fear, and hammer out on the anvil of doubt.*

It takes courage to keep on keeping on when you'd rather just quit. We can't let discouragements, failures, or regrets shackle our minds. Everyone suffers setbacks and no one advances on an unbroken front.

Psychologists call these stalemates plateaus in the curve of learning. If you had enough spunk to get started, you have enough spunk to keep going when the going gets tough.

THIRD
Consistency Completes Commitment

Abraham Lincoln is an inspiring example of consistency of purpose to become an educated man and a competent speaker. With only one year of schooling, he educated himself. He walked twenty to thirty miles to hear the dynamic speakers of his time. Then he went home and practiced, imitating their style and delivery. He talked to the trees, to the crops, to customers in Jones' Grocery Store in Gentryville, Illinois. He talked to people on the street if they'd stop long enough to listen. He joined debate clubs and spoke up every chance he had. Although he was painfully shy, ungainly, awkward, and insecure, he reached such a high level of eloquence he is still considered one of the most compelling speakers of all time.

"They can conquer who believe they can," said Ralph Waldo Emerson. "He has not learned the first lesson of life who does not every day surmount a fear."

Lincoln would have made an ideal member of Toastmasters International, whose members overcome fear by conquering it. They attend regular meetings, deliver their speeches, and improve them by applying the constructive criticism of their colleagues.

They follow Benjamin Franklin's advice, "Resolve to perform what you ought; perform without fail what you resolve." Dynamic speakers get that way performing before audiences—not sitting in them.

Lincoln's curiosity and courage to learn would have made him a remarkable scholar, but it was his consistency of purpose to become an eloquent speaker that made him one.

To become the polished speaker you want to be, you need curiosity, courage, and consistency of purpose. If you start with curiosity, you generate the courage to overcome obstacles and by consistently striving to become a poised and confident speaker, you become one.

Chapter 13

Improving Your Self-Image and Self-Esteem:

Get Involved with Yourself

"Remember always that you have not only the right to be an individual; you have an obligation to be one. You cannot make any useful contribution in life unless you do this."
—Eleanor Roosevelt

You can never love another person until you first love yourself. Most of us are so committed to conformity, though, that we neglect the individuality that makes each of us a one-and-only person in the universe. Most of us start out in life thinking we're okay; then adults begin pointing out defects, weaknesses, and failures to keep us from becoming egotistical. What a load of insecurity we carry through life because of feelings of inadequacy and inferiority.

So common are these feelings of inferiority that the Public Broadcasting Corporation published a booklet, *Celebrate Yourself: Six Steps to Building Self-Esteem* that offers advice for anyone seeking more self-confidence. The main character, Nitpicker, is an obnoxious potato who acts as the "internal critic" we all carry around that nags and scolds us all the time. This meanie is a carryover from childhood when we lacked the ability to evaluate information and believed whatever we were told. Unfortunately, most of what we remember is negative.

"I was a loner as a kid," Kevin Costner said, "small, gangly, with big feet—a real late bloomer. Even today, I wish I were smart... more disciplined...and better read." So even worldwide accolades, fame, and fortune aren't always enough to silence the internal critic.

FALLING IN LOVE IS A TRANSFORMING POWER

Remember your first love? You were ten feet tall and strong, courageous, exciting, generous, positive, energized—a conqueror. What a pity we don't still perceive ourselves the same way. We probably don't have any more faults or shortcomings today than we did when we were in love and felt lovable.

Whatever you love, you cherish and protect. When you love yourself, you take pride in your appearance and abilities, protect your health and safety, and present yourself in the best possible way.

A person who has high self-esteem is cheerful, outgoing, positive, unselfish, loyal, and cooperative. The person with low self-esteem can be sarcastic, abusive, uncaring, and insensitive. These people are either consumed with self-hatred or so needful of attention they go to any lengths to humiliate and downgrade others in order to pull them down to their own level.

People who think they're OK can accept their mistakes, inabilities, and shortcomings as normal and universal. They don't hold grudges or dwell on the mistakes of others. They are able to forgive themselves as quickly as they forgive others.

YOU ARE A SOMEBODY: BELIEVE IT!

You wouldn't be where you are, doing what you do, accomplishing what you accomplish if you weren't a *somebody*. Sure, you're not perfect (who is?), you've gone off the track now and then (who hasn't?), and have a long way to go (who doesn't?). Congratulate yourself on how far you've come and what you have already accomplished.

Someone's sure to argue, "Getting involved with yourself is the sure way to become an insufferable egotist." Not so. It's possible, but highly improbable. Most of us underrate rather than overrate ourselves.

LOVING YOURSELF MAKES YOU SECURE

You don't need to climb on a soapbox, beat your breast, and pro- claim to the world how wonderful you are. You are comfortable in your own skin, content with your own life, accepting of your own shortcomings, proud of your own abilities. You are yourself—and glad of it. You can forgive yourself as you do others.

The people with poor self-image and low self-esteem stand on a wobbly pedestal and fall off with the slightest bump. Then, of course, it's not their fault:

"She made me do it."
"He doesn't like me."
"He lied to me."
"She stole all the glory."
"My wife is too extravagant."
"My husband doesn't understand my needs."

The I-me-myself complex comes from lack of self-love, not too much of it.

FIVE WAYS TO LOVE YOURSELF MORE

1. Every night, analyze the things you said or did that were unbecoming. Determine who or what motivated you to exhibit such behavior. Don't agonize over this, but learn from it.

2. Hang this sign over your mirror and read it every morning:

   Today I will value myself as someone special and act that way to become even more so.

3. Visualize the way you want to look, act, and present yourself. It's the *only* way to actualize what you see in your mind's eye.

4. Replay your mental tapes of the times you've captivated an audience, and take pride in your ability to do so.

5. Resolve to present yourself to your colleagues and family as the *somebody* you know you are. Loving yourself will make you lovable.

When author-editor Frank Moore Colby said, "Self-esteem is the most valuable of the emotions," he was emphasizing the importance of holding yourself in high regard with appreciation and approval. Why shouldn't you enjoy your own respect?

When someone pays you a compliment that you know is sincere and deserved, why depreciate it by saying, "Oh, that wasn't anything really," or some such inane remark. Such a remark detracts not only from your accomplishment but also from you as a person. And you also deflate the person who is honoring you. If you deserve the acclaim and honor, simply smile and say, "Thank you. How kind of you to tell me."

Being involved in a love affair with yourself doesn't mean you thump your chest and shout your worth to anyone who will listen and those who don't. It's a quiet appreciation for who and what you are, gratitude for your potential, and respect for yourself that give you the confidence to perform to the best of your ability.

RAISE YOUR SELF-ESTEEM WITH PRAISE

Dr. Johnathon Freeman, in his book, *Happy People*, reported the answers to the question, "What makes you happy?" that he had asked thousands of people in an effort to find out what people really did want. Is it fame, fortune, power, beauty, success? No! The single most-reported answer was "to like myself."

David Viscott, author of *Risking*, wrote, "The more you love yourself, the less dependent you are on others." Asking people what they think about you is a waste of time. Your friends won't tell you the unvarnished truth; your enemies are only too willing to tell you how homely, awkward, ineffective, or boring you are. And who wants their opinions, anyway?

FIVE WAYS TO RAISE YOUR SELF-ESTEEM

1. Concentrate on *five* qualities you admire in others and cultivate them in yourself—qualities such as persistence, honesty, kindness, joyfulness, compassion, and thoughtfulness.

2. Compliment at least *five* people every day on some quality they possess that you admire, thus focusing attention on your own lack of (or desire for) these characteristics.

3. Every night list *five* things you did or said that bolstered your self-esteem and enhanced your self-image. Pat yourself on the back for having said or done them.

4. Study the people with poise and confidence to learn what makes them that way.

5. Spend at least *ten* minutes before going to sleep visualizing yourself as an effective, compelling, charismatic person. This is no time to be modest or self-deprecating; whatever you see in your own mind's eye will eventually be seen in every other eye.

Chapter 14

Tapping Into Your
I-Can Power:

It's the Power to Put You Over the Top

"Nothing in the world can take the place of persistence. Persistence and determination alone are omnipotent."

—Calvin Coolidge

"You may be disappointed if you fail, but you are doomed if you don't try," said Beverly Sills.

Your I.Q. may be that of a genius, but without a high level of I-Can power you will never be the winner you could be.

Edmund Burke, British statesman, said, "Never despair. And if you do despair, work on in despair." Notice the active verb *work*, which is what I-Can power is all about. It is the perserverance to keep on when it's the last thing you want to do.

Many a race has been won by a runner with bleeding blisters; many a game has been won by a pitcher with a painful shoulder; many a compelling communicator has stood on trembling legs to present his or her ideas. What these winners all had was a high level of I-Can power. It's I-Can power that makes the impossible possible.

Someone once said, "Moses should have been given another commandment: THOU SHALT NOT QUIT." One man who also believed that no one should quit was Fridtjof Nansen, Norwegian explorer and statesman, who, with his companion, became helplessly lost in the forbidding arctic wasteland. As they staggered through the blinding whiteness across the bleak and desolate terrain, Nansen's companion said, "I can't go. I simply can't go on."

And he lay down in the snow and died.

Nansen, however, was endowed with I-Can power. "I can take one more step. I can take one more step," he kept saying. And that's just what he did. One stumbling step after another, he kept staggering on until he came upon the American rescue party sent out to find the lost explorers.

History is full of miracles created by people who had so much I-Can power they tackled impossible tasks and achieved amazing results. For example, Josiah Wedgwood spent 15 years trying to create the first English china teacup; Charles Goodyear experimented 28 years to vulcanize rubber; Thomas Edison made 10,000 attempts to create an incandescent lightbulb before he succeeded; John Creasey, mystery writer, collected 743 rejection slips before he got one word into print; Willie Mays went to bat 26 times before he got his first home run in the major leagues; Oscar Hammerstein had five flop shows before *Oklahoma*, which ran for 269 weeks and grossed $7 million on a $23,000 investment.

Dick Francis, English novelist, was once a jockey riding for the queen in steeplechase races. He suffered a severe accident and was forced to retire. Then he began an entirely new career that resulted in the publication of some three dozen best-selling novels.

"People always asked where I got the courage to take those hurdles in steeplechase competition," Francis said. "I just told my horse to throw its heart over the hurdle, and I'll follow right behind."

Norman Vincent Peale, famous speaker and writer, wrote in one of his books, *The Power of Positive Thinking for Young People*, about a young circus performer who was being trained on the trapeze bars high in the circus tent. One day the coach said, "Today you work on the high swings without a safety net."

"Oh sir, I can't possibly do that! I'm not ready to work without a safety net."

"Nonsense!" shouted the coach. "Of course, you can. All you have to do is throw your heart out on the wind and your body will follow."

IT'S HOW YOU HANDLE WHAT HAPPENS TO YOU

Losers hide behind excuses to justify their failures. "I've never had any luck," "My parents wouldn't let me," "She's jealous of me," "I never get the breaks," "Everybody's against me."

Winners, in contrast, take adversity or handicaps and bend them to their demands. Glenn Cunningham, the great runner, had so much I-Can power he defied every obstacle and achieved impossible dreams because he made them possible.

When he was a boy, Glenn was so badly burned in a schoolhouse fire the doctors said he would probably never walk again, let alone run. But Glenn paid them no mind. He began following the plow back and forth across his father's Kansas farm leaning on the handles for support. After agonizing efforts, he developed enough strength to walk behind the plow without hanging on. Then he started hobbling as fast as he could, stumbling along the furrows. When he was able to, he started running and kept right on running until he set world records in the one-mile competition.

Michelanglo knew all about I-Can power when, in his 80s, he lay on his back on scaffolds high in the Sistine Chapel painting the ceiling with brushes strapped to his wrists because his hands were so crippled with arthritis.

History books and biographies are full of accounts of people who have excelled and conquered with I-Can power. President Harry Truman was a haberdasher; Paul Gauguin a stockbroker; Thomas Paine a corset maker; Sean Connery a bricklayer; Richard Burton a miner; Elvis Presley a truck driver; Andy Williams a barber. You can't pick up a magazine without some story about a person who's risen above and beyond certain trials and tribulations.

TOO MANY OF US ARE OUR OWN WORST ENEMIES

Many losers are similar to the patient who complained to his therapist about his bad luck and failures. After listening to the litany of "poor-me" stories, the therapist said, "I'm afraid I have some bad news for you. I think you're allergic to yourself."

All of us operate within the limitations of heredity and environment, but we can control our responses to restrictions, conditions, or parameters.

People who drag through life wondering why everything is such an effort may be like the man struggling to keep his wagon moving along a dusty country road. When he saw an old farmer sitting on a fence post, he asked, "How much longer is this hill I'm trying to climb?" The old man laughed, "Hill? 'T'ain't no hill, mister. The back wheels on your wagon are off."

Losers drag through life with their back wheels off because they're blaming everyone else without checking their own equipment—attitudes, reactions, ingenuity, ambition, determination, persistence, and I-Can power.

People who make mistakes and can accept them become winners somehow, someway, sometime. A young college student who fouled up a major football game wrote home to his father, "Our opponents found a big hole in the line...and the hole was me." That young man had enough insight to recognize his mistakes, take responsibility for them, and would later profit from knowing when he was wrong.

ACHIEVEMENT DOESN'T HAPPEN OVERNIGHT
It's easy to watch professionals in action and sigh with envy wishing to be like them. We admire Nancy Kerrigan, Scott Hamilton, Michael

Jordan, Billy Graham, David Copperfield, Colin Powell, Bill Cosby, Jay Leno, Robert Schuller, and others. Never overlook the hours and hours of hard work and endless hours of practice these successful people have put in to get where they are. Never forget for a moment that they didn't spring from their high chairs into the limelight. There were grueling hours of struggle and defeat after defeat, but they overcame all with I-Can power developed to the highest level.

Every child should be told the story of *The Little Engine that Could*, and then made to memorize it and use it as a lodestar to victory. As the little engine huffed and puffed its way confronting the challenge of reaching the top of the mountain, it kept saying, "I think I can, I think I can, I think I can." When it finally reached the top, it sighed with satisfaction, "I thought I could, I thought I could, I thought I could."

That's the kind of I-Can power that puts a little engine on the peak of a mountain and people over the top. It's what puts compelling and charismatic communicators on stage facing an audience with composure and confidence.

Even practiced and professional speakers experience trepidation and nervousness before facing an audience. My friend Marcus Bach was a world-renowned religious researcher who spoke before huge audiences around the world. He confessed, "I never step onto a stage without being tense and suffering stage fright. But I believe a certain amount of nervousness contributes to a heightened ability to draw on strength and confidence."

Napoleon was only five feet, two inches tall, but he thought of himself as a giant among men and conducted himself accordingly. He faced all challenges with supreme confidence in himself. He once said, "When you go to take Vienna—take Vienna." The rest of us could use that as a motto too, when we're faced with even the smallest challenge.

Trust your I-Can power to give you the confidence and composure to throw your heart out to the wind when you step before an audience, and you'll be surprised how your inspiring words will follow and make you the compelling communicator you want to be, can be, and will be.

POINTS TO REMEMBER

◆ Memorize: THOU SHALT NOT QUIT

◆ I-Can power moves mountains.

◆ Look to achievers for inspiration.

◆ Conquer fear of speaking by talking to everyone who will listen everywhere you are.

◆ Use *The Little Engine that Could* as an example of achievement.

◆ Remember: If you throw out your heart on the wind you will follow.

◆ I-Can must go steady with faith in yourself to make an indomitable pair that always succeeds.

◆ People with I-Can power automatically believe they will achieve their goals.

◆ I-Can power has more power than I-wish or I-want.

Chapter 15

How to Make
Yourself a Winner:

Become What You Want to Be

"I do not think winning is the most important thing. I think winning is the only thing."

—Vince Lombardi
(football coach)

Arthur Miller wrote in *Death of a Salesman*, "He's a man out there in the blue, ridin' on a smile and a shoeshine—a salesman has got to dream, boys." Without dreams of who you want to be and what you want to accomplish you won't sell yourself or your ideas to anyone.

Dreams are visions of what we would like to be, like to have, and like to enjoy if we are to make our lives meaningful to ourselves as well as to others.

What makes one person a dreadful bore? What makes someone dynamic, fascinating, convincing, and magnetic?

BECOMING WHAT YOU WANT TO BE

To become the person you want to be you need to understand the principles behind the creation and then apply them to everyday behavior.

An article in *Cosmopolitan* magazine several years ago by T. P. James spelled out the process in simple terms; "Understanding the psychology of the self can mean the difference between success and failure, love and hate, bitterness and happiness. The discovery of the real self can rescue a stumbling marriage, recreate a faltering career, transform victims of personality failure. On another plane, discovering your real self means the difference between freedom and the compulsions of conformity."

Finding your real self means locating powers of communication you didn't know you had that will astound not only the people around you but even yourself.

You have valuable ideas to share or you wouldn't be where you are today. And you have ambition and expectations or you wouldn't be seeking ways for self-improvement and searching for secrets to more success. What you may lack is the realization that you have to awaken the sleeping genie within you that's waiting to obey your bidding and to make your dreams come true.

RELEASE THE BEST IN YOU

People under hypnosis do and say things that astound them when the spell has been lifted. Sometimes, the realization is of greater significance than the person expected. Dorothea Brande, in her book *Wake Up and Live*, wrote that she was able to draw on talents and abilities she never realized she had after witnessing a demonstration on hypnosis. She said, "If people are able to release talents, abilities, powers, and behavior under hypnosis, why couldn't they tap into this source of power by self-hypnosis?" So she set about hypnotizing herself on the assumption that she could tap into ideas and abilities she had neglected to investigate. She hit upon the idea that if she acted *as if* she could do or have the things she wanted, she would actualize them. And it worked!

Within a year, she was not only increasing her production as a writer but discovered she had a talent for speaking—something she had always hated to do and had shown no previous aptitude for doing.

Self-hypnosis isn't necessary if you can convince yourself that your best self lies not in your mind but in your mind's eye.

You will never become better looking, more effective, more dynamic, or more charismatic until you *see* yourself this way in your mind's eye and *believe* you can become that wished-for person.

LET YOUR GENIE OUT OF THE BOTTLE

Your subconscious mind is the most willing, capable, dependable, and innovative genie you could ever know. It is eager and capable of obeying your slightest command or realizing your impossible dreams.

The problem, however, is that this genie has no ability to discern right from wrong, success from failure, real or unreal. It operates without making judgments or weighing options. Because it is non-judgmental and unable to differentiate truth from fiction, it delivers exactly what you direct it to deliver. So you are the creator, director, and producer of whatever scenario you program into this power station—your genie or subconscious mind.

Napoleon shaped history to suit his ambitions. One of his major goals was to conquer Corsica. He drew up detailed war maps and arranged his armies in his mind to take advantage of the weather, terrain, and fortifications, working them together as well as separately to win imaginary battles. He *rehearsed* these battles over and over in his mind, adjusting and readjusting his mental images in such vivid detail that it was impossible to fail. Napoleon might have resisted giving his subconscious mind credit for his success, but that was what he was doing through mental imaging.

THE PROOF IS IN THE PUDDING

A friend of mine who was a novice on skis perfected his skill when he was marooned in the Vietnamese jungles. He confided, "I sat in those miserable, bug-infested, steaming hideouts suffering every kind of physical and mental torture. I saved my sanity by visualizing myself skiing down slopes on a packed-powder surface, perfecting my skills by facing imaginery hazards, emergencies, and accidents. I'd mentally choose the right skis for the variables in the snow, see myself waxing them and then performing like a pro. When I got back home and on the slopes again, I couldn't believe how my performance had been improved by all that mental visualization."

Dorothea Brande tells in her book, *Wake Up and Live*, how to concentrate on the idea that you can achieve your desired goal by avoiding all thoughts of past failures. She said, "The psychologist F.M.H. Myers changed my life with his discussion of 'purgation of memory,' by which you ignore all past failures. I decided I would act on the assumption that it was impossible to fail. Within a year not only had my production increased but my sales, too."

Another surprising result was her newfound ability to perform on stage as a successful communicator. "I not only discovered I *enjoyed* lecturing but had a talent for it...something I had never before thought possible."

YOU DESIGN AND RECREATE YOUR NEW SELF

Dr. A. Nathaniel Branden, author of *The Psychology of Self-Esteem*, wrote, "The first step is to realize from the core that we alone are responsible for what happens to us. When we grasp that concept and build it into our thinking and acting, we can rebuild our self-image and create within ourself a feeling of self-worth...a recognition that we are entitled to the best things in life."

Gene Tunney almost lost his first fight with Jack Dempsey as well as his heavyweight championship because of mental imaging. He said, "I had nightmares seeing myself bleeding, mauled, and helpless sinking to the canvas and being counted out. Right then, I was losing the match. But when I realized that I was thinking about the fight in the wrong way, I started to redesign my mental attitudes. I stopped reading all the papers that predicted Tunney was slated to lose; I stopped thinking about Dempsey as victorious. I began seeing myself punching him out and handling the ferocity of his attacks."

LEARN TO ACT, NOT REACT

Most of us have been conditioned by parents, authority figures, the environment, jobs, and education to react to situations and people much like Pavlov's dog began salivating at the sound of a bell. We often *react* without taking time to decide how we really want to *act*. And there is a vast difference. Reacting rests on the powers of others; acting gives *us* the power. Much of our behavior results from our *reactions* that make us feel victimized, helpless, and out of control. What we need to do is take a few seconds to decide how we are going to act, not react, to the situation.

Harry Truman was under tremendous stress during his presidency with all the added burden of World War II demanding world-changing decisions. His colleagues were amazed at how well he kept his stability without losing his composure or showing the effects of stress.

He once explained, "Well, it's like this. I have a foxhole in my mind where I go to recoup and organize my thoughts." He withdrew from the situation and decided how to act rather than react to the demands or decisions needed. Thus, he avoided being stampeded into quick decisions or escaping pressure from associates demanding immediate action.

UNREALIZED GOALS CREATE MENTAL DISTRESS

We are born to be goal-strivers, so we are miserable when we have no goals or can't reach the goals we have. People are disconsolate and feel constantly out of control if their goals seem to be lost or forever pushed beyond reach because they lack the power to achieve them. Most of these distressing problems arise because we are reacting to our environment rather than acting to keep control. We lose sight of what we really want and must do to achieve our goals because we are victims of our submission to situations, people, or environment. One way to get control of ourselves and the situation is to retreat to a *mental foxhole* for a few moments to gain perspective and to energize our spirits.

HANDLE A CRISIS WITH A WHAT-IF ATTITUDE

Walter Pidgeon, a popular 1950s actor, was performing on stage for the first time and was paralyzed with fear. He said, "I was scared to death. I was a terrible flop all during the first act. I thought I'd never survive. Between the first and second acts, I thought about what would happen if I really was a flop. Then I knew I had to take control of myself. I took the what if attitude that saved me. I thought if I was a total failure at acting I could always find something else to do. It wouldn't be the end of the world if I couldn't make it on the stage."

He went back for the second act and turned in a stunning performance. When he began to act instead of react by taking a so-what or what-if attitude he relaxed, his subconscious took over, and his genie produced a triumph.

Very few things are a matter of life and death. It's the way we look at a crisis that determines whether it will control us or we'll control it. Successful performers admit to being terrorized by stage fright, but they've learned to control it by deciding to act before an audience rather than react from fear of an audience who didn't come to witness failure by the speaker.

TEN WAYS TO BUILD SELF-CONFIDENCE
Dr. Denis Waitley, a motivational instructor and the author of numerous books on building self-esteem in order to succeed, contends that business and professional people will never advance to

their highest potential until they visualize what they want to become. Until you see in your mind's eye, you won't see in reality. His students are indoctrinated with this belief.

Trying to get to the top before you're ready to function at that level is akin to putting the cart before the horse. You first have to prepare yourself mentally and emotionally to cope with the demands top-level executives face every hour of every day before you can hope to arrive at that spot. Even after you've prepared yourself for the demands of an executive position, you have to be able to handle communication of all kinds effectively, convincingly, and winningly.

Here are Waitley's ten commandments that he declares will turn you into the convincing communicator you must be before you can achieve your goals and then maintain your control over them.

Even though his suggestions may sound ordinary and repetitious of advice you have heard before, the truth is always worth reviewing.

1. Always dress like a winner.

2. Answer the phone in a clear, confident manner.

3. Accept compliments with poise, "Thank you. How nice of you to say that."

4. Every night make a list of things you're grateful for that happened during the day.

5. At meetings, sit in front of the room and take an active part in discussions.

6. Walk everywhere with a proud and confident posture.

7. Set your standards of behavior by the rules observed by gracious and refined people.

8. Speak with self-confidence but respectfully to everyone.

9. Make a list of short-range and long-range goals.

10. SMILE, SMILE, SMILE!

POINTS TO REMEMBER

◆ Realize you have a powerful genie—your subconscious mind—that will work for you.

◆ Control your imagination so it does not control you.

◆ Design a blueprint of what you want to become—a success.

◆ You were born a goal-seeker; set your goals for success.

◆ Plan your goals in advance and move steadily toward them.

◆ Memorize the ten commandments for daily behavior and guidance.

◆ Never forget: Your must *see* what you want in your mind's eye before you can make it happen.

◆ You can make yourself the winner you want to be and can be.

Part IV

Broadening Communication Horizons

Chapter 16

◆

Acquiring Communication Skills:

A Three-Step Plan

"Each honest calling, each walk of life has its own elite, its own aristocracy based on exellence of performance."

—James B. Conant

Richard Bandler and Joe Grinder, experts in neurolinguistics, had their lectures compiled into a book, edited by John O. Stevens, titled *Frogs into Princes*. Using the analogy of a frog who became a prince of communication, the authors set forth their precepts for changing from an inept, incompetent, bumbling speaker to a fluent, articulate, persuasive prince of communication.

The results that Bandler and Grinder have achieved reveal that all speakers can improve their verbal and presentation skills by following these three steps:

STEP 1
Concentrate on Your Audience

Most people are more concerned with what they feel, think, and want than with what others feel, think, and want. You must *connect* with your audience through the humanness that links us together and makes us fellow travelers with the same goals, aspirations, hopes, expectations, and needs. It's the only way you can develop rapport that will make your audience want to listen to you.

STEP 2
Be Alert for Feedback Clues

Negative feedback:

> *Are people fidgeting or whispering?*
> *Are they reading books or papers?*
> *Are they looking around or out the window?*

Positive feedback:

> *Are people sitting quietly?*
> *Are they smiling back at you?*
> *Are they maintaining eye contact?*

It is imperative that you pick up and respond to these clues and know how to cope with the negative feedback. If you lose people's attention and don't get it back immediately, you're in trouble. The longer inattentiveness goes on, the harder it is to regain control. If you lose it altogether, you might as well sit down—or go home.

STEP 3

Capture Attention at Once

The first moments of your presentation are called "uptime." Your entire attention should be on the audience—not yourself. You can't spend a minute wondering if your jacket is buttoned up right, if your hair is staying put, or whether your clothes are appropriate. It's too late to do anything about it anyway. Your obligation is to your audience, because they are there waiting for your performance.

If for any reason you find yourself unprepared, or sense your audience isn't ready for your speech, you have to adapt.

Once Franklin Roosevelt was sitting on a platform as the keynote speaker for a high school commencement ceremony, when he realized that what he had intended to say wouldn't be appropriate after all.

He stood up and smiled. "I've just decided that what I came here to say to you won't do at all. So I'm going to put aside my notes and talk about something more suitable to the occasion."

Which he did, to the delight of the entire audience.

Let's suppose you're not quite as eloquent as FDR, and you find yourself in a situation where you decide that what you'd intended to say wouldn't be appropriate. What can you do?

◆ Choose another introduction that will relate to the audience.

◆ Eliminate controversial material that might be antagonistic. If you can't because it's important to your speech, then be as diplomatic as you can.

◆ Use anecdotes that are more suited to the occasion.

HOLDING YOUR AUDIENCE

Accomplished speakers can read between the lines and pick up on misleading clues. They don't assume that just because one woman is staring at them, she is engrossed and fascinated. Her mind could be a hundred miles away, or she could be asleep with her eyes open. The man fumbling in his pocket for a pen may be trying to fool you into thinking he's going to take notes, when what he really intends to do is doodle or write a note to his neighbor.

An attentive audience is usually quiet and focused on you. If something or someone causes a disturbance, it can upset the entire audience. Coughing or sneezing can start an epidemic that sweeps the room. Someone dropping a book can create more excitement than you do.

RECAPTURE ATTENTION IMMEDIATELY

This is where you have to be flexible and adapt. You must improvise and ad lib. What can you do to recapture the audience's attention? Try these things:

◆ Come out from behind the podium and walk around the platform, or even the room in extreme cases.

◆ Stop talking and fumble through your notes or briefcase, or search for your glasses in pockets or among your papers.

◆ Stop talking and stand still until you've created such an ocean of silence that your audience stops what it's doing to wonder what you're doing.

◆ Ask someone in the audience to answer a question.

◆ Ask for a show of hands in response to a question.

Admittedly, it takes confidence to do anything so drastic, and you may feel like a fool using such unorthodox methods to regain attention. But anything is better than losing control of your audience.

A speech professor at the University of Chicago once broke every rule in the book to demonstrate how nontraditional a speaker can be. He paced around the room, broke chalk and threw it to the floor, sat down in the middle of the room with the students, perched on his desk, and waved his arms like windmills. He was exciting and spellbinding. None of us could take our eyes off him, for we were immersed in his dramatic performance.

WHOSE FAULT IS IT WHEN THINGS GO WRONG?

Usually it's yours. The professional and reputable speakers accept responsibility for communication breakdowns. They say, "Look for the key in disagreements or misunderstandings. Usually it's my fault for one reason or another. Either I'm not listening intently, or I'm insensitive to negative feedback clues."

Be an actor—not a reactor. Those speakers whose presentations fall far short of the mark and fail to move their listeners are usually so self-centered, they are oblivious to an audience's response. They are deaf and blind to anything except their own self-involvement. They often have tunnel vision, so they see only what's obvious. They prepare a speech (even memorize it!) and then deliver it without once observing the audience's response. They sabotage themselves all by themselves—and usually don't even know they've been sabotaged.

There is nothing mysterious about those speakers who have confidence in their abilities to influence an audience. There is no more mystery to applying neurolinguistics to your speeches or presentations than there is to applying arithmetical principles to arithmetic problems. Most of us are able to achieve what we want, if we learn how to go about it. Now that you know and can apply these concepts of effective communication, you, too, can acquire the necessary presentation skills, and with your newfound poise and confidence, become a privileged member of the finest group of speakers and leaders.

Chapter 17

◆

Winning Loyalty Through Communication Skills:

Understand What People Want and Need

"Loyalty is one thing a leader cannot do without."

—A. P. Gouthey

Successful and enduring relationships are not accidents—they are created and maintained by knowing how to get along with people. Winning the support and loyalty you need to succeed doesn't happen by chance or circumstance. It develops because you generate loyalty by your respect for the ties that bind us all to one another.

People who can't get along with associates and clients are the first to be fired when cutbacks are made, and many times just because they are so disagreeable to be around. At least one-third of our lives are spent in close relationships with people we work, live, or socialize with. If you don't understand how to enlist the support and cooperation of your coworkers, you are going to find it hard to realize your goals. If you fail to produce what's expected of you and are unable to develop and maintain good relationships among your colleagues and people you deal with as clients, you will be pegged somewhere toward the bottom of the upward-mobility ladder, or asked to step off entirely.

There is only one way to win loyalty and support from the people you work for and with: *Understanding the humanness in us all*. The only way you reach that understanding is through communication.

YOU CREATE YOUR RELATIONSHIPS

Dr. O. A. Batista wrote in his book *Commonscience in Everyday Life*, "No matter how smart a person is or how hard that person may work, he can't get anywhere alone. On the job, it's important to possess an aggressive personality, but it's far more important to keep this aggressive personality on a leash, preferably well hidden under such outward qualities as persuasion, genuine friendliness, good taste, and diplomacy."

You don't have to be a hypocrite, or weather vane shifting with every opinion in an effort to please everyone. You become tactful, diplomatic, and sincere dealing with people because you understand and respect what ties us together.

Your success everywhere depends on your associates, coworkers, and superiors. You gain their loyal support by creating bridges of understanding among them. The burden, however, rests entirely on you as the communicator (giving and receiving ideas) to see that exchanges are accurate, complete, and understandable.

USE THE ATTITUDE THAT ALWAYS SUCCEEDS

"Your ideas are important to me," or "I need your ideas on how we should approach this problem," you will find more often than not they will be happy and eager to cooperate and help you. How do you respond when someone appeals to you for help or advice? If you're made to feel important and necessary to the success of a project, you are going to become an enthusiastic team player who wants to help bring about the success or achieve the goal the leader wants.

Here are four ways to win loyalty and promote cooperation that will help you get what you want:

1. **Ask for advice.** Most employees like to feel they know something about the job they have. Ask questions. "Could you give me some suggestions for dealing with our department manager who I know is going to oppose this policy I want to present to the board next week?"

2. **Ask for assistance.** "Would you give me a hand with this new computer? I hear you're an expert analyst and I need help figuring out how to operate this machine."

3. **Ask for ideas.** "You've had a lot more experience handling customer complaints, so could you give me an idea of how to talk to this irate woman who wants to return a dress that was on sale and is clearly marked nonreturnable?" "Have you any idea how I can handle this month's report so I'll impress that new auditor?"

4. **Ask for support.** "You know I'm bringing up a controversial plan for reorganizing the structure of our company, and I'm afraid I'm going to meet a lot of resistance. Do you think you could give me some support when I propose this to senior management next week?"

The other side of the coin is the "I-am-more-important-than-you-are" attitude that authoritative persons project without even realizing that it does nothing but alienate the very people they need to help them.

Here's an example. Jackson is an attorney who frightens clients by the way he answers the phone. He barks, "Well, what do *you* want? Speak up. I'm in conference, and time is money to a lawyer." Who wouldn't bristle with that brusque, impatient, undiplomatic greeting? The only thing that keeps his clients loyal are family ties and a long-time association with people who try to understand his irritating manner.

Jackson's at a loss as to why he can't keep new clients and he's losing some of the oldtimers who are getting tired of being treated like an annoyance or an unwanted idiot.

It's little wonder that Benjamin Franklin was such a successful diplomat. He said, "The way to convince another is to state your case modestly and accurately, then add that you, of course, could be mistaken about it. This causes your listener to listen to what you have to say, and like as not, turn about to convince you about it since you appear to be in doubt. But if you go to him in a tone of positiveness and arrogance you only make an opponent out of him." And opponents never make loyal and supportive people who help you succeed in achieving your goals or destinations.

LEARN TO SMELL SMOKE

A lawyer friend often says, "Well, it's been a rather trying day. It seems as though I spent my time putting out little bonfires in the office." How sensitive are you to the clues people around you throw out to alert you there's trouble brewing? If you are perceptive, you can put out little blazes before they become raging infernos. How do you smell smoke before you see the flames?

Nonverbal Communication.

Actions are loud indicators of what's going on without a word being said. Take Dorothy, for instance, who came to work at the senior center last Tuesday with a scowl on her usually smiling face. She started slamming desk drawers, banging the coffee machine, snapping at her coworkers, and generally behaving in an altogether abnormal manner.

Joe, who is the supervisor of the center's employees, picked up on the clues that indicated trouble was brewing. He said "I can spot dissension as quickly as I pick up a rattle in my car. I knew something was terribly wrong with Dorothy, so I called her to my office and had a quiet talk with her. I found out she was furious because the substitute who was to take her place while she went on vacation had canceled out. I knew Dorothy had made expensive and elaborate plans for her vacation, so I could sympathize with her feelings. I told her we'd get another substitute right away and she could continue planning to take her vacation when she'd been promised the time to go."

Joe put out a little fire that could have blazed out of control and would have reflected on the entire department. Had he ignored Dorothy's behavior, her negative attitudes and actions would have not only infected the whole area but would have been inflicted on the people coming to the center.

It's wise to confront any dissension head on as Joe did and stamp out a little fire before it becomes a bonfire of a problem.

DEALING WITH PROCRASTINATORS

Procrastinators can throw a monkey wrench into an entire operation and not only slow down production but sabotage it entirely.

Procrastinators are indecisive because they are fearful of making the wrong decision, so they avoid making any. Adlai Stevenson was such a procrastinator, he drove Eleanor Roosevelt to practically tearing out her hair because he wouldn't declare his intentions to run for president. He solved his dilemma by waiting until it was too late to enter the race, thereby taking the decision out of his hands.

Procrastination is a bad habit, but it can be broken. Fear of almost everything keeps procrastinators wavering back and forth until it's too late to take action, which is what they've avoided doing all the time. They fear to act for fear it will work against them in some way, but it's this fear to act that puts people in self-constructed prisons.

You can deal with foot-draggers if you understand that it is fear causing so much indecision. How do you handle procrastination?

1. Insist that some decision is made.

2. Refuse to dwell on past mistakes.

3. Force a decision by overruling controversy that's only a stall for time.

4. Don't accept repeated excuses to delay decisions.

A famous industrialist who groomed young men for top-management jobs said, "I force them to make decisions. Wrong or right, any decision is better than none. I refuse to allow procrastination to slow down production or delay progress."

Of course, like everything else that can be carried too far, sometimes it's wise to let an issue simmer for awhile before a final decision is made. But simmering doesn't mean allowing the pot to burn up because you can't decide when the simmering is done.

LEADERS CAN ALSO BE TEAM PLAYERS

Management prizes team players for they keep the wheels rolling and progress developing. If you can relate to your colleagues in such a way that you create harmony, progress will naturally result. Team players put the welfare of the company, organization or project ahead of personal gains or desires. Management looks with benevolent eyes on employees who know how to win cooperation and support among their fellow workers.

When you develop *perceptivity*, you can inspire your associates to work with you. When you cultivate *sensitivity* you relate to your colleagues because you understand their fears, hopes, aspirations, longings, and insecurities are similar to yours. When you understand that we are all vulnerable, you discover how alike we all really are.

YOU WIN LOYALTY AND SUPPORT BY COMMUNICATING

A personnel director in a large midwestern bank expressed his attitude toward the question, "What do you consider is the most important characteristic a person should have to succeed in the banking world, or any world, for that matter?"

He replied, "The most important attribute anyone can have is the ability to get along with people. The second is having a keen sense of knowing how to communicate. We can teach people banking procedures, but if they can't relate to their associates and our clients, they won't win loyalty for the bank. Anyone who can't handle people by knowing how to communicate with them on all levels doesn't last very long around here.

"The people we advance to executive positions have the ability to communicate. When I hire a new person, I give him or her five directives I expect to be observed. More people are let go through misunderstandings than are ever fired because they can't do the work. We overlook mistakes or minor discrepancies, but we *never* overlook an indifferent or discourteous employee who hurts our customers' feelings or upsets other employees by tactless remarks or lack of respect."

Here is his list of the five essentials in the art of communicating:

1. **Always be courteous.** Never ruffle feathers or tread on toes. Never be indifferent, impatient, or rude to a client.

2. **Don't overdo flattery.** People are suspicious of anyone who gushes or fawns over people. We believe in praising our people but doing it with diplomacy and tact. We expect our employees to do the same with one another and our customers.

3. **Protect the dignity of everyone.** Bruising an ego or crushing feelings can make an enemy of a loyal customer and lose the business. Furthermore, a person whose feelings have been hurt will tell friends and relatives about it and turn them against our bank.

4. **Have enough self-confidence to admit mistakes.** Admit you don't know everything. Admit you're "green," for green things are growing things.

5. Don't throw your weight around. Acting superior is how the weak and insecure person tries to bolster a weak ego. It's a cover-up for feelings of inferiority that only draw attention to them.

YOUR SUCCESS ANYWHERE DEPENDS ON PEOPLE

You must have the support, loyalty, and cooperation you need to help you get where you want to go. Regardless of your goals, you will never reach them without the loyalty and support of people who want you to succeed.

There's an old saying, "A cork always finds its own level," which applies to people, too. Like cream that insists on rising to the top of the milk bottle, you can insist on rising to the top. You have to know how to rise and then have the stay-with-it power to remain there when you get there.

POINTS TO REMEMBER

1. Understand what people want and need.

2. Know how to win cooperation.

3. Smell smoke and put out little fires.

4. Make decisions without procrastinating.

5. Be a team player as well as a leader.

6. Follow the rules set up by top management.

Chapter 18

Talking Without Words:

Using and Understanding Body Language

"Speech is power: to persuade, to convert, to compel."

—Ralph Waldo Emerson

It's a sobering thought to realize that only about half of what passes for communication takes place with words. The other half is a silent language taking place with gestures, facial expressions, postural changes, and images. Unless you become informed and can read body language, you're communicating with only half the information you need to be effective.

When the frontier of kinesics opened the study of how our feelings and emotions are expressed through bodily actions, a whole new type of communication developed.

BODY LANGUAGE IS A NONVERBAL EXPRESSION OF IDEAS

A politician, for example, who's trying to woo a group of union members with whom he secretly disagrees will expose his feelings in body language. He may pound the podium with a clenched fist or hold a clenched fist against his side or in a pocket even though he's shouting his approval of the union's position. If he's scowling, has a red face, is strident in his delivery, he may be secretly despising the union's position on tariffs, while declaring, "You are the backbone of the country's welfare, and I applaud your attitude toward imported competition." Any listener clued into body language will pick up the nonverbal disapproval and base his support on what he's not hearing rather than what he is.

TWO BROAD BODY LANGUAGE CATEGORIES

An effective communicator who's alert to nonverbal language can judge the approval or disapproval of an audience by watching how they sit and change postures.

Open and receptive:

A person open to your suggestions or advice will unconsciously sit or stand with the body at ease and perhaps bending forward toward you. The hands may be held outward or upward on a table or lap, the head will nod now and then with silent approval, friendly smiles will come and go on a relaxed face. All these open gestures reveal a supportive and acceptive attitude.

In any audience, address these people as often as possible by smiling or looking at them. You need as many of these open members of an audience as possible. They unconsciously influence the less supportive listeners and can be helpful in turning a hostile group of listeners into a supportive one.

Closed and resistant:

An audience made of listeners who are bitter, opposed, resentful, or hostile will be impossible to handle until the closed minds are changed one way or another. The faces will be set and grim, bodies held in rigid positions often leaning as far back in the chairs as possible, legs tucked back under the chair or crossed tightly or even entwined, their hands may be clenched in their laps or sides, and arms crossed across their chest. Some closed persons will show resentment by looking out the window, reading a paper or book, rolling their eyes heavenward, even grunting with disapproval or muttering under their breath.

Unless you can convert this type of listener with a closed mind into an open and receptive person, you might as well sit down or go home. There are ways to cope with such an obviously closed person that can be successful:

1. Ask the person to clarify her position, so you can understand what she's thinking.

2. Propose an alternative and ask for opinions.

3. Change the subject temporarily or approach it from another angle.

Sometimes you can appeal to a dissenter who's expressing disapproval without speaking a word by directly asking for an opinion or alternative. This may defuse the situation or produce a new idea that may be better than your own. If the agitator creates enough contention, the audience itself will be able to quiet the dissenter.

Don't be so rigid and unyielding that you can't or won't accept suggestions. Never underestimate the ideas coworkers or employees bring to your attention. You may need to revise your own thinking, much as that might upset you.

Whoever or whatever is alienating the people you need to reach, your objective must be handled with finesse and diplomacy. Beating against closed minds is as futile as beating your head against a steel door. The door will survive; your head won't. And once you've lost cooperation and support, you're out of the game.

POSTURAL IMAGES

Just as minds falls into roughly two major groups, postural images can be defined in three major groups. Each of them provides insights into how people are feeling and thinking even though they aren't aware of how their bodies are talking. When you learn to pick up the negative feedback provided by these images, you have another insight into how people are responding to you and your ideas.

Mirror Image.

In a group of people there are usually dominant members who are influential in swaying others to their way of thinking or feeling. Concentrate on the ones who are open and receptive. Keep watch on the dissenters with closed minds whose body language reveals their disapproval or resentment. Keep alert to their postural changes to see if they are relaxing and mirroring the postures of the receptive members of the group. Experienced and effective presenters know the dissenters in the audience must become receptive and agreeable to the proposals they're being asked to support if success is to be achieved. Keeping close watch on the postural changes within a group gives you the feedback you need to be effective.

Gender Image.

Young people tend to imitate the leaders in any group, falling in with their postural changes as their minds accept the leader's ideas.

Example: Young men wanting to appear sophisticated and worldly often assume the "broken four" posture by sitting with one ankle on the knee of the other leg. Somehow, they think this image projects confidence and a casual control of the situation.

Young women wanting to appear confident, friendly, and open to male attention may assume what's known as the gender posture.

Example: A young woman open to male attention will cross and recross her legs, slip the heel of a shoe off and on one foot, sit with her body turned toward the young man, twist a strand of hair around one finger, and lean forward with her hands turned outward or palms up in her lap.

These postures may be assumed unconsciously or knowingly, but they can usually be interpreted as postures that reflect inner feelings.

Barrier Image.

These postures are loud and clear: Don't present your ideas to me; you can't convince me no matter what you suggest; my mind is made up; don't confuse me with the facts.

The closed-minded person is mentally sitting behind a wall with a wide moat between you. All the postural changes associated with a "don't-come-near-me" attitude will express themselves with the way such people sit, stand, and move.

Unless you remove these barriers, whatever you say and do will be ignored, distrusted, or disobeyed. You can't succeed with any group if the barriers are too rigid and resistant.

Pick up the negative feedback from such barrier images and change your approach or quit talking.

BE SENSITIVE TO THE UNIVERSALITY OF GESTURES

All around the world, people communicate in foreign languages without understanding a word. They do it by reading body language. People who are blind or can't speak the language still communicate with common and worldwide gestures.

For instance, think of what these gestures convey: the shrug, the wink, the scowl, the smile, downcast eyes, a shuffling walk, a thumbs up or thumbs down, the circle formed with the thumb and forefinger, the waving hand, the crossed eyes, eyes rolled heavenward, the smirk, the outstretched hand. The more gestures that are used and understood in a given exchange, the greater becomes the communication going on in silence.

NONVERBAL LANGUAGE IS MORE DEPENDABLE THAN VERBAL

Spoken language is made up of jargon, slang, innuendoes, vocabulary limitations, ethnic connotations, mispronunciations, cultural differences, speed impediments, and many other elements. Communicating on the verbal level is like walking through No-Man's Land with mines endangering every step.

In contrast, body language is the same everywhere with only a few deviations in cultural practices, which can be understood if attempted. You will be surprised to discover how much more you can learn about a person by reading body language in addition to hearing verbal language.

HOW TO BECOME AN EXPERT IN NONVERBAL COMMUNICATION

Start watching people on buses, in restaurants, on street corners, on TV talk shows, at the movies, in advertisements. Try to interpret what they're saying without words by evaluating postural changes, eye movements, gestures, and facial expressions. The more you concentrate on silent communication, the more expert you become in reading people like a book.

An actress being interviewed by a reporter said, "Unless you can pick up on the body language going on in this movie, you won't understand half of what's going on. It's very subtle but very important."

When you become adept at reading unspoken language, you will become more at ease everywhere and become so sensitive to people's feelings, you will gain the reputation of being a mind reader. Actually, that's just about what you will become.

Remember that at least half of what's going on in the communication process is going on without a word being said.

POINTS TO REMEMBER

◆ Body language makes up at least 50 percent of communication.

◆ Be aware of cultural differences in body language for better understanding in all situations.

◆ Learn to read people by studying them in all types of situations.

◆ The more effective you become in reading body language, the more effective a communicator you become.

◆ Verbal language is a No-Man's Land too dangerous to encounter without understanding body language.

◆ The more you understand nonverbal language, the more you control your audiences in both formal and informal situations.

Chapter 19

◆

Attaining and Maintaining Your Credibility:

Four Ways to Gain or Recapture It

*"The only way you can motivate people
is to communicate with them."*

—Lee Iacocca

Communication today is changing so rapidly and involving so much new technology and devices for sending messages faster and more often that we may find it more difficult than ever to send and receive information accurately.

The information superhighway will someday funnel through one pipeline all communications systems: telephone, fax, cable, and broadcast television signals as well as other computer networks worldwide. The network will have videophone channels over which you will be able to teleconference with colleagues across the country. Microsoft Chairman Bill Gates predicts that the cost of videoconferencing, like that of other computer-driven services, is going to drop as other technological and communications costs have. Whether you will make presentations over the information superhighway or in person, though, you must be a credible com-municator.

When you think of how difficult credibility is to achieve at present, it boggles the mind to think what may happen in the future when communication becomes faster and takes place more often without opportunities for clarification or in-depth discussion.

What passes for communication during an ordinary work day is usually a mishmash of ideas being exchanged by word of mouth and written communiques. Yet effective communication doesn't just *happen.* If the ideas from your mind are not received accurately and exactly by the listener, communication breaks down.

Credibility is lost most of the time for four reasons:

1. The language is not specific.

2. The directives are fuzzy, incomplete, or inaccurate.

3. The messages are misread, misinterpreted, ignored, or lost.

4. The senders and receivers are not qualified communicators.

Credibility in communication is achieved only if both the sender and the receiver understand the four components of communication:

What to do
When to do it
How to do it
Why to do it

If these four requirements aren't met, your credibility is on the line. Never underestimate how much you are judged by how well and convincingly you communicate your ideas to others.

CREDIBILITY DEPENDS ON COMMUNICATION SKILLS

Your ability to be a persuasive and effective communicator requires two activities: *Sending and receiving messages*—both oral and written.

As a sender: You must be concise, accurate, thorough.

As a receiver: You must be attentive, open-minded, listening.

Communication is a two-way street with ideas going back and forth between minds with all kinds of obstacles, distractions, and detours threatening communication. Neither a sender nor a receiver can be a passive participant in the transfer of ideas.

Because so many directives, requests, and expectations are transferred through writing, you are always in danger of not sending or receiving the correct meaning of what's being transferred.

YOUR CREDIBILITY IS ALWAYS ON THE LINE

Credibility is made up of intangibles as well as tangibles—the way you walk, dress, enter or leave a room, stand behind a podium, answer your telephone; how and where you park your car, how you speak to subordinates and superiors, handle your records, and so on.

Your actions speak volumes to the people you work and live with. If your actions are shouting one thing and your words something else, you are written off as noncredible.

Example: Leonard manages a large real estate office with agents coming and going throughout the day. Communication between him and the salespeople depends on the written messages he leaves on their desks or hands to them as they come and go. Leonard's notes are so garbled and incomplete that they are usually disregarded by the recipients who can't depend on them. Everyone complains about the lack of communication, but Leonard complains bitterly because he accuses his associates of never reading their messages or ignoring them if they do.

Leonard's credibility has been lost through his indifference to it. But he blames everyone else for the lack of communication taking place in the office. Leonard's credibility may not be under scrutiny much longer for there is a movement gaining strength to see that Leonard is removed and the aggravations suspended.

Sometimes, credibility is lost without it being your fault. Interoffice communication isn't always reliable. Your messages can be mislaid, misconstrued, ignored, lost, or thrown away. If you sense your directives aren't achieving what you intended or need, it's up to you to find out why. Gaps in credibility can result in errors, loss of clients, misunderstandings, profit loss, and insubordination.

YOUR CREDIBILITY IS YOUR PROBLEM

The higher you climb in an organization, the more responsibility you assume, and the harder it may be to get your ideas and requests heard and acted upon. If you are communicating ineffectively, you will lose credibility as well as support and respect. When you sense something is disrupting your communicative efforts or someone is carelessly or deliberately thwarting your efforts to establish confidence and support, use the Socratic method of asking for opinions or suggestions: Talk to people one-on-one, or as a group if you suspect you're out of step with the majority of your colleagues, and question them:

> *Do you have a better way to handle this situation?*
> *Do you understand what I'm trying to accomplish?*
> *Are you convinced that our goals are for mutual gain?*
> *What suggestions do you have to correct this problem?*

The more rapport you can establish with coworkers and employees, the more successful your communicative process will become.

Remember, you won't make any progress at all if you come at someone with a fist.

If you're not being taken for a credible and dependable person on a day-to-day basis, an audience made up of peers isn't going to be any more impressed with you on stage than they are off.

Another reason for failed communication and loss of credibility is "selective listening" by you or people you talk to. Most of us are adept at turning off our listening when we hear disagreeable directives or criticism of our efforts, appearance or behavior. We can become downright deaf when our prejudices or loyalties to religious or political beliefs are attacked.

To remain credible, avoid these five common barriers that cause selective listening:

1. closed minds

2. personal prejudices

3. stereotyping

4. inadequate vocabulary or unfamiliarity with jargon

5. insecurity and lack of self-esteem

Monique came from France as a computer analyst in a satellite tracking station. She is bright, competent, cooperative, and very efficient. But she is lonely, isolated, and more or less ignored by her coworkers. Why? Her inability to communicate with them because of her limited grasp of innuendoes, jokes, slang, and double meanings of words make her an outsider. Her credibility as a computer whiz is being challenged simply because she is unable to communicate with her associates. Unfortunately, they can't make allowances for her limited vocabulary and help her understand their Americanized language.

Whenever you're confronted with situations where resentment and resistance can destroy your effectiveness and credibility, it's your responsibility to see if any one or more of the five barriers to communication is blocking understanding and your credibility.

HOW TO REINFORCE YOUR CREDIBILITY

Be sensitive.
Concentrate on reading negative feedback from body language, disinterested listeners, and resentment to your ideas or your status.

Reinforce oral communiques with written messages.
If you're responsible for promoting new or radical ideas, be aware that hearing them may go in one ear and out the other or that minds are turning off resisting the entry of new ideas. Even though you've established credibility in the past, the introduction of new policies or different programs are often difficult to absorb or accept.

If you're presenting something you fear may have a negative response, reinforce your talking with writing (after the oral presentation) and see that everyone involved gets the same copy with as much tangible evidence as possible.

Be specific.

State exactly *what* you want done, *when* you want it done, *how* you want it done, and *why* you want it done. Sometimes explaining the importance of what you're asking for expedites the completion of the work as well as making it better. Remember always that some people need the reinforcement of *seeing* in addition to *hearing* directives or requests.

Much of what goes wrong in communication is the responsibility of the communicator who fails in the initial exchange of information to clarify the purpose and importance of the message.

Whenever a bottleneck or a derailment of information occurs, it's your responsibility as the communicator to find out why, how, and where the accident or deliberate attempt to sabotage your communication occurred and why.

Use familiar terms and examples.

Sometimes communication fails when unfamiliar terms or references are misconstrued, ignored, or treated as irrelevant. Always be aware that when you are introducing new ideas, new options, controversial issues, or unwanted new policies you are going to encounter resistance. Use familiar terms and examples to get your point across. You will gain credibility by using terms your audience can understand and relate to.

BE ALERT TO CREDIBILITY GAPS

The more your credibility is in question, the harder it is to establish it as a given and dependable quality. If you develop sensitivity and perspective, you should be able to pick up clues, shifts in reactions, changing attitudes, a cooling off of interest. All these indications that distrust or disinterest is occurring need to be rectified as soon as you detect them. Go to the source, if you know it, for information and help. If you don't know the why or wherefore of disinterest, set about immediately to find it.

Four ways to gain or regain credibility:

1. *Be alert* to shifts in attitudes or actions that signal trouble.

2. *Be patient* and receptive to anyone coming to you with new ideas, radical departures from the norm, or complaints.

3. *Be open-minded* and willing to listen to unsolicited ideas or suggestions. Being dogmatic will weaken credibility.

4. *Be a good listener*. One of the greatest assets anyone can cultivate is listening. It's hard to know if someone is really listening to you or just pretending to listen, but you can determine when *you* are listening. You can reap great dividends from concentrated, receptive, and unwavering listening.

BE AWARE OF THE TONE IN COMMUNICATION

Many times, credibility is threatened by the tone of voice, the rate of speaking, the emphasis on words with emotional impact, the attitude conveyed by voice inflection. Messages can be distorted simply by the *tone* in communication.

For example: Joe is a farmer who could neither read nor write, so when he received a letter from his son, he took it to his neighbor and asked him to read the letter. It was a reasonable and well-written letter such as any respectful son would write to his father. The son asked about the crops, the weather, the price of corn, and so on. Then he ended the letter with a request for money explaining that he was short of cash.

The neighbor—who secretly was jealous of Joe because he could neither read nor write but owned 100 acres of the best land in the county—was impatient and irritable and read the letter quickly without color or emotion in his voice. Joe listened and was obviously angered at what he thought was an inconsiderate and callous attitude of his son as expressed by the tone of his letter.

"And I should send him money? To hell with him!" he shouted.

Several weeks passed, and the father couldn't get his son's letter out of his mind. It just didn't seem right that his son would write such a cold and demanding letter. So he took it to another neighbor. This farmer owned 150 acres of the "black gold" farmland known as the best soil in the county. He admired Joe for having done so well without benefit of an education and for having raised a good son. He was neither impatient nor irritable and read the letter with a soft voice and sympathetic tone. When he finished, Joe had tears in his eyes.

"Ah, now that's different," he said in a loving voice. "Of course, I'll send him whatever money he needs."

The tone of the message can create failure or success and decrease or increase the favorable impact of whatever you want to accomplish. Boosting your credibility and bridging gaps in understanding can both be accomplished using the proper tone in your communication.

YOUR CREDIBILITY NEEDS CONSTANT ATTENTION

It takes constant diligence and self-evaluation to maintain credibility once you've attained it. It can slip away on tiny, silent feet and never be missed until you discover how ineffective you've become.

When you achieve credibility, keep it by monitoring it with caution and concern. If you suspect you may be losing some of it through a gap in communication or misinterpretation of your communiques, repair the rift in understanding as soon as possible before your credibility is weakened or lost altogether.

Credibility requires stability and dependability. No matter how old you become, how disillusioned you are at times, nothing is more heartening than depending on someone who is always dependable. Nothing provides more confidence than turning to a stable person in this unstable world of shifting values.

Credibility is a hard won and difficult prize to capture and then protect. Nothing will pay greater dividends than attaining and maintaining your credibility.

CHERISH YOUR CREDIBILITY

1. Create it.

2. Honor it.

3. Maintain it.

4. Guard it.

POINTS TO REMEMBER

◆ Credibility rests on intangibles as well as tangibles.

◆ Remember the four ways to gain or regain credibility.

◆ Credibility depends in large part on communication skills— speaking and listening as well as writing and reading.

◆ Credibility requires stability and dependability.

◆ Take charge of your credibility to keep it.

◆ Credibility requires constant attention.

Chapter 20

Managing Mental Imagery:

Success Is All in Your Mind's Eye

"Castles in the air—they're so easy to take refuge in. So easy to build, too."

—Henrik Ibsen

Building castles in the air may sound fanciful, but it's just another term for daydreaming or mental imagining that has been proven to be an effective way to make you a more compelling communicator. In today's high-tech world, daydreaming might be better understood if it were called managing mental images. Whatever it's called, daydreaming brings astonishing results.

Everything that ever was, is, and will be was first an idea, a plan, an intention, or a vision. Nothing is ever *realized* until it has been *visualized*. Dynamic speakers know the power of mental imagining, which is seeing in your mind's eye that which you want to become, achieve, conquer. Every successful platform speaker, negotiator, minister, lawyer, performer, or leader, became that person *mentally* before becoming that person in reality. The process is nothing new. It's just plain, old-fashioned daydreaming.

Daydreaming helps people learn, concentrate, renew their energies, and achieve better interaction with their families, audiences, and coworkers. Daydreamers are better able to handle stress. And if you think facing an audience of one or one thousand doesn't create stress, you are a rarity, a born orator, or have never faced an audience.

"A little nervousness is good," writes Malcolm Kushner in his bestseller, *Successful Presentation for Dummies*. All dynamic speakers, on stage and off, have managed stress, stage fright, insecurity, and timidity by programming themselves to overcome these defeating emotions. And most of their success has been through structured and managed mental imagining—scientific daydreaming or building castles in the air.

1. *You connect with your inner self.*
Author Dorothea Brande says daydreaming is a time when you revitalize yourself. "It seems as though the mind gives a great sigh of relief at the liberation and stretches itself to its fullest limits."

Successful inventors, artists, writers, and public speakers have all mastered the art of daydreaming, whether they call making the connection with their inner selves an inspiration or flash of insight.

2. *You put the subconscious mind in control and your conscious mind on hold.*
You begin meandering up and down the avenues of your mind recalling incidents, experiences, hopes, dreams, and ambitions that you have realized in the past and that you hope to realize in the future. Within your subconscious mind are files and files of stored material that can be retrieved at will, reviewed and rearranged.

Daydreaming becomes a process of reorganizing past events or hoped-for achievements into new patterns something like the way a kaleidoscope arranges and rearranges the same flecks of color.

DAYDREAMING IS AN ART

Winners see themselves winning whatever contest, competition, or game they're entering. They not only see themselves in the winner's circle but eulogized as heroes. Kushner writes, "Imagine that they give you a standing ovation and rush the stage to carry you out on their shoulders." Great achievements start with a picture held in your imagination until it becomes the real thing instead of a figment of your mental imaging.

Jack Nicklaus daydreams before every golf tournament to get the "winning feeling" he derives from *visualizing* himself as a winner. He said, "It gives me a line to the cup just as clearly as if it's tattooed on my brain."

DAYDREAMING IS A PROVEN SKILL

When the Olympic contenders were en route to Stockholm, Sweden, in 1912, the coach monitored the exercise periods of the athletes with unrelenting insistence. One day, he saw Jim Thorpe just sitting with his eyes closed and doing nothing.

He stormed, "Jim, why aren't you out there with the others practicing and exercising? You can't accomplish anything just sitting around."

"Oh, Coach, I'm practicing. I'm practicing. I'm visualizing myself winning everything in every event I'm going to compete in."

Which, of course, is just what he did. He won the pentathlon and then the decathlon to become one of the all-time greats.

Bob Beamon, gold medalist, who held the world record in the long jump from 1968–1991, said, "You have to keep visualizing yourself in your mind's eye and hold that image in your mind every night before you go to sleep."

WHY DAYDREAMING WORKS

It's a scientific procedure that never fails. Dr. Maxwell Maltz, plastic surgeon and author of the best-selling book *Psycho-Cybernetics*, wrote, "Your nervous system can't tell the difference between an imagined experience and a real one. In either case, it reacts automatically to the information you give it from your forebrain. Your nervous system reacts appropriately to what you think or imagine to be true."

Daydreaming must be controlled. You can't just sit down and start a willy-nilly daydreaming session letting stray thoughts or images come and go as they choose. It's not a period of escaping from reality. Daydreaming is a *selective process*. You must retrieve and replay mental images of your past successes, achievements, and noteworthy performances, and conjure up images of future successes. Thoughts or memories that replay failures or losses must be controlled like wayward puppies. Winners *refuse* to dwell on any unpleasant or unsuccessful incidents or performances.

DAYDREAMING IS A SCIENTIFIC PROCESS

You control your mind in direct proportion to your ability to concentrate on what you select from your storehouse of information to review. Repetition creates impressions that become deeper and more entrenched with review. You become what you concentrate on becoming.

Let's take, for instance, an unknown chess player who defeated the world-famous chess champion, Jose Capablanca. When Alex Alekhine upset the champion, the event was likened to an amateur flyweight boxer defeating the world heavyweight champion.

Here is how Alekhine did it. He hid out in the country three months before the match. He gave up smoking and drinking, went on a strict diet, and followed a rigorous exercise schedule. He spent hours every day sitting in an easy chair playing mental chess. He set up an imaginary chess board with imaginary chess pieces and then proceeded to play the game using every gambit he'd heard of to checkmate his imaginary partner time and time again.

He so conditioned his mind that when he sat down to actually play, he simply drew on his subconscious mind to give him the insight and skill to win game after game. His defeat of the world champion was so unexpected it created a furor in the chess world.

Then, take Arturo Schnabel, world-renowned Austrian pianist who toured the United States in 1921. He admitted that he had hated to practice so much he had quit touching the piano after seven years of lessons.

He practiced his compositions by mentally playing them over and over in his mind without touching a finger to the keyboard.

Successful men and women in all walks of life have used mental pictures and mental rehearsal to achieve success.

DAYDREAMERS ARE PERSISTENT

Skip Ross, in an article in *Possibilities*, wrote about a man in Southern California who had his heart set on a house he'd seen. Although it was out of his price range financially, he was determined to have it. This daydreamer believed so strongly in his ability to visualize what he wanted and see it realized that he set his plans in action. He issued 100 invitations to friends for a house-warming party one year in the future to be held in his new home.

Then, he set about daydreaming—and also pursuing the dream by acting. He approached banker after banker trying to negotiate a loan, none of whom gave him any encouragement. Finally, he persuaded a banker to read a letter he planned to write to discuss why he should have this particular house. This time he was successful.

One year later, on the day he had set for his party, he opened the door to his dream home and welcomed his 100 guests to the party.

MAKE DAYDREAMING A DAILY RITUAL

The process is as old as mankind. Long before modern times, in Proverbs 13:12, we read, "Hope deferred makes the heart sick, but when dreams come true at last, there is life and joy"

The time spent daydreaming can be the most important time of the day. But it must be a structured and respected period of time.

Establish a daydreaming place.

Find a quiet place where you won't be interrupted with people, telephones, noise, and confusion. Hang a mental sign over this place that reads, "Quiet! Daydreamer at work."

Go to this place every day.

If possible, go at the same time and stay the same length of time. Sit in a comfortable chair and close your eyes. Then imagine a blank movie screen dropping in front of your face. See yourself walking onto a stage in front of this screen as you want to walk onto the speaker's platform in front of your audience. Visualize yourself dressed in becoming clothes, groomed to perfection, and exuding confidence from every pore. See yourself facing an entranced audience listening to every word you are speaking with a compelling voice and manner. Then visualize yourself walking off the platform to the thunderous applause of a fascinated audience.

Continue this imaginary scenario, repeating the procedure over and over, changing your appearance in your mind's eye and improving on your posture and delivery as you impress upon your subconscious mind how you will act, look, speak, and think when you *are* the compelling communicator you will become.

Success depends on attitude and time spent.
What you achieve depends in direct proportion on the time spent and the seriousness of your intentions.

PRESENTATION PROJECTS POWER
A famous Russian prima ballerina, forced to retire because of age and failing health, started a dancing school for little aspiring ballerinas.

When the lessons began and the little girls lined up at the bar for their exercise period, the teacher would shout the command "PRESENT YOURSELF!"

Instantly, every little spine stiffened, every shoulder lifted, every head raised as though connected by a string to the sky, and every leg tightened to a perfected stance.

As the teacher checked every girl's posture, she would repeat the same admonition, "Performance depends on presentation. You will never be better than you appear to be."

What powerful advice that teacher was giving her students.

DAYDREAMING BECOMES REALITY
No vision, dream, plan, idea, or image ever materializes until it is taken from the abstract and put into the concrete. Whatever you want to see realized in your life must first be visualized. And there is no more productive way to become the compelling communicator you want to be than seeing yourself as that person in your daydreaming sessions.

POINTS TO REMEMBER

◆ Daydreaming is scientific.

◆ Make daydreaming a structured process and a part of your daily routine.

◆ Daydreamers who picture themselves as winners become winners.

◆ Success as a communicator is directly related to effective daydreaming.

◆ Add written directions to your mental ones to reinforce the daydreaming process.

◆ Daydreaming is not an avoidance of reality but a connection to it.

◆ Present yourself as you want to be remembered and respected.

Chapter 21

Afterword:

Your Effect on Your Audience

"The tongue is the heart's pen and the mind's messenger."

—Bahya Ibn Paquda
(11th century Spanish poet)

After all the words telling you how to present yourself and your speeches with poise and confidence, here are some afterwords to take with you.

Never forget: You are a catalyst whose audiences will never be the same after hearing you talk to them.

The pen is mightier than the sword, but the spoken word is mightier than both. Orators can charm an audience; demagogues can delude their constituents; con men can defraud the trusting; propagandists can inflame a nation; pedagogues can put an audience to sleep; and politicians can change a nation's laws.

English poet Alfred, Lord Tennyson pointed out the danger of an orator's art of illusion: "Charm us, orator, till the lion looks no larger than the cat."

With ability comes responsibility. The more charismatic you become, the more catalytic you are. Never forget the person you influence today may go forth and influence 10,000 people tomorrow.

The art of illusion is perfected by orators who seek to influence audiences by appealing to the emotions rather than the minds of the listeners.

When the Jewish poet Moses Ibn Ezra, writing in the 11th century, wrote, "The worst of men is he whose tongue is mightier than his mind," he was categorizing orators who seek to influence audiences so they will be motivated to act or react to the suggestions they are hearing.

Orators fascinate, overwhelm and seduce audiences who leave wondering what has happened on stage that leaves them bewildered and confused. They're aware that they've witnessed a performance but are not sure what it was all about.

They are like two old men who listened to a politician discoursing at length at a Fourth of July picnic. When he finally sat down, one man said to the other, "That feller can sure talk purty, can't he?"

"Yep." said the other, "Know what he was talkin' 'bout?"

"Nope! Not a clue."

Perhaps, after all is said and done, Anne Morrow Lindberg may have put it best when she said, "Good communication is as stimulating as black coffee and just as hard to sleep after."

If you leave your audience so aroused they are unable to sleep, unwilling to sleep, and unneeding to sleep, you will have become what you wanted to be—an effective and dynamic communicator who makes presentations with poise and confidence that have impact, credibility, and effectiveness.

SUGGESTED READINGS

1. Allen, Steve. *How to Make a Speech*. (McGraw-Hill Co., 1986).

Preparing and performing speeches for unusual situations, using humor effectively, handling the actual performance.

2. Anderson, James B. *Speaking to Groups: Eyeball to Eyeball*. (Wyndmoor Press, 1989).

Three keystones to the right stuff, a dozen dangers and how to cope with them, handling intangibles, using visuals.

3. Bandler, Richard and Grinder, John. *Frogs Into Princes*. (Real People Press, 1979).

Using neurolinguistics for effective presentations, making your speeches "exquisite communication," making uptime count in grabbing an audience's attention.

4. Bowling, Evelyn Burge. *Voice Power*. (Stackpool Press, 1980).

Making effective presentations, finding and using your hidden voice potential, techniques of making power speeches.

5. Bristol, Claud. *Magic of Believing*. (Prentice-Hall Inc., 1976).

Developing your potential, building self-esteem, learning to be successful in personal and professional relationships, building your self-confidence with mind power.

6. Brown, Lillian. *Your Public Best*. (Newmarket Press, 1989).

Putting your best appearance on stage (makeup, clothes, hair), developing voice appeal, handling the media, making the most of meeting rooms, platforms, and TV.

7. CPB Personnel. *Celebrate Yourself: Six Steps to Building Your Self-Esteem*. (Corporation for Public Broadcasting, 1990).

Building self-confidence through applied procedures. Learning to have faith in yourself, becoming the best you can be.

8. Flacks, Niki and Rasberry, Robert W. *Power Talk*. (Free Press division of Macmillan, 1982).

Waking up your vocal and physical powers, applying theatrical techniques to give you stage presence, using actors' devices.

9. Lieberman, Gerald F. *3,500 Good Quotes for Speakers*. (Doubleday, 1983).

Quotations for special occasions and inclusion in speeches.

10. Linver, Sandy. *Speak and Get Results*. (Summit Books, 1983).

Discovering and organizing the purpose of your speech, reaching your audience by developing your own style, handling various business situations, making presentations with confidence and effectiveness.

11. Mooney, William, and Donald J. Noone, Ph.D. *ASAP: The Fastest Way to Create a Memorable Speech* (Barron's, 1992).

12. MacMahon, Ed. *The Art of Public Speaking*. (G. P. Putman, 1986).

Finding the purpose of your speech, organizing and preparing for delivery, knowing how and when to use humor, relating to your audience effectively.

13. Nelson, Robert. *Louder and Funnier*. (Ten Speed Press, 1985).

Making a fear map to assess your fears, overcoming stage fright, handling an audience, conquering feelings of inadequacy.

14. Ochs, Donovan J. and Anthony C. Winkler. *A Brief Introduction to Speech*. (Harcourt Brace Jovanovich, Inc., 1979).

Basic fundamentals of preparing and presenting a speech, recognizing types of speeches and how to organize and prepare them: good beginner's guide to speech making.

15. Orben, Robert. *2000 New Laughs for Speakers: The Ad-Libber's Handbook*. (Gramercy Publishing Co., 1978).

Conveniently classified jokes to fit all subjects, advice on how to choose and use jokes in your speeches.

16. Winokur, Jon (compiler). *The Portable Curmudgeon*. (New American Library, 1987).

Clever compilation of witty and appropriate anecdotes for many occasions, literary quotations as well as contemporary epigrams. Small book can be tucked into coat pocket for ready reference.

INDEX